Arbor promises to be a great resource for those who desire to grow deeper in their relationship with the Lord. Throughout this discipleship training curriculum, Kaylee Farn has demonstrated passion, wisdom, and an impressive knowledge of scripture. I found myself moved by the stories she shared about her personal encounters with the heart of God. Ever since meeting Kaylee, she has shown remarkable humility, integrity, and an infectious fire for Jesus. My wife and I consider it an honour to call her a spiritual daughter. There is no doubt in my mind that God is raising her up to be a prominent voice who will inspire and impact many.

Luc Niebergall

Founder and President of *Royal Identity Ministries*

Author of *Pioneer*

Co-Author of *Revival Secrets*

ARBOR

Kaylee Farn

Scripture references in this book are taken from the New King James Version®, copyright © 1982 by Thomas Nelson, Holy Bible, New International Version®, NIV®. Copyright © 1973, 1978, 1984, 2011 by Biblica, Inc.™ Used by permission of Zondervan. All rights reserved . New Living Translation, copyright ©1996, 2004, 2015 by Tyndale House Foundation. Used by permission of Tyndale House Publishers. All rights reserved. The Passion Translation®. Copyright © 2017, 2018 by Passion & Fire Ministries, Inc. Used by permission. All rights reserved.

ARBOR

Copyright © 2021 by Kaylee Farn

Cover Design: Todd Toews

ISBN: 9798450714578

Imprint: Independently published

All rights reserved.

Printed in Canada

ACKNOWLEDGMENTS

To my spiritual parents, Luc and Sophie Niebergall who have shown me the love of the Father in endless ways. There are not enough words to describe my gratitude for you both.

To Soraya Prajzler for being the friend that sticks closer than a brother.
Proverbs 18:24

Introduction

INTRODUCTION

I wrote the Arbor Curriculum with the intention of starting a discipleship training program for a summer camp. Over the span of eight months, I took time to pray and fast about what this could look like and how it could impact the lives of those who came in contact with it. When covid19 arrived and the summer camp ended up closing for the season, I was confused as to why the Lord so clearly had asked me to be faithful in writing this curriculum. After the last devotional was done, I didn't look at it again until about a year later when a friend of mine shared her dream of starting a discipleship training school in her church and how she wanted to write a curriculum that sounded exactly like this very one I had written and forgotten about. Shocked, I pulled up my work to see if it was similar to her vision, and of course, it was! It was at this moment that I knew I had to finish what I started and get it published so that more people could use it if they felt led. I believe that many lives will be impacted through these simple teachings of how to grow in friendship with God.

I titled this curriculum Arbor because of its prophetic symbolism. An arbor is a garden structure on which plants and vines can grow. They are specifically intended for climbing plants which need support to keep growing and to reach full maturity. Climbing plants typically must twine around a support in order to continue growing upward. As they are attached to this support, they can be trained to go where you want them so that they will become the most beautiful they can be and to be perfectly placed around the arbor. When climbing plants grow vertically, they are able to be used the most efficiently and it becomes easier for them to bear fruit. The produce that comes from these plants is kept much cleaner than when grown on the ground and they are able to breathe better around the arbor, minimizing disease. When the climbing plants are fully grown around the arbor, it adds much beauty to the garden.

In a similar way, when we are planted, rooted, and even fruitful in Christ, we must learn to intertwine ourselves with Him, to abide in His Presence and cling to His support. Growing up in Christ is rarely easy, but the end product is beautiful and stands out among the rest of the garden. In order to reach full maturity, keep growing, become fruitful and experience life abundantly, we must lean on Him as our support so that we can continue growing upward towards the Father. As we yield to Him, He will guide us where we need to go and teach us how to live for Him.

John 15:5 says *"I am the Vine, you are the branches. He who abides in Me, and I in him, bears much fruit; for without Me you can do nothing."* He wants us to become the best versions of ourselves in Him, but we cannot do this if we don't learn to abide and stay close to Him in friendship. If we remain in Him, He will use our lives effectively and help us to bear much fruit. As we fix our gaze on Him, and cling to His hand, He will help us along the way and do immeasurably more than we can ask or imagine in and through our lives. I pray that you would learn to yield to God and allow Him to prune you as you are planted, rooted, and fruitful through friendship with Him.

"Now to Him who is able to do exceedingly abundantly above all that we ask or think according to the power that works in us."
Ephesians 3:20

DEVOTIONAL 1
PLANTED: WHO IS GOD?

I t is extremely important that we know who God really is, and what He is like in order for us to truly know who we are in Him. Below we will explore the characteristics of the Father, the Son and the Holy Spirit to be able to better understand His nature and how we relate to each Person of the Trinity. I will conclude with a personal encounter with the Father, a prayer to follow, and some questions for self-reflection.

Jesus Christ

J esus is the Word of God in flesh form as well as the Father's beloved Son. He was sent to the earth to bear the weight of our sin and die on the cross so that we could be made right with God forever! He is fully God and fully man and has broken down every wall that separated us from God so that we can now have direct access to the Father at all times. He is the foundation of the Church in which we build all things upon and He will come back to earth again as a victorious King to establish a new heaven and a new earth!

♥   He stands in 24/7 intercession on our behalf so that all things will work out for our good and His glory
♥   The Mediator that is defending us before God and has forgiven us our sins

Ephesians 2:14 (TPT) *"Our reconciling "Peace" is Jesus! He has made Jew and non-Jew one in Christ.*

By dying as our sacrifice, He has broken down every wall of prejudice that separated us and has now made us equal through our union with Christ."

Ephesians 3:15 TPT *"The legal code that stood condemning every one of us has now been repealed by his command."*

♥ Before Jesus died on the cross for us, we were all destined to condemnation because of the law that had to be followed perfectly in order to remain in right standing with God.

♥ All have fallen short of the law and require a Saviour.

♥ When Jesus died on the cross, the legal code that condemned mankind was removed and God gave us the free gift of salvation through grace, rather than works.

Ephesians 2:13 TPT *"Yet, look at you now! Everything is new! Although you were once distant and far away from God, now you have been brought delightfully close to him through the sacred blood of Jesus – you have actually been united to Christ!"*

♥ With the Kingdom of God now within us, we are able to receive everything that Jesus has made available to us through His perfect sacrifice

Ephesians 2:16-17 TPT *"Two have now become one, and we live restored to God and reconciled in the body of Christ. Through His crucifixion, hatred died. For the Messiah has come to preach this sweet message of peace to you, the ones who were distant, and to those who are near."*

♥ We have been reconciled to God to coexist with Him in harmony, unhindered by the law that separated us.

Ephesians 2:18 TPT *"And NOW, because we are united to Christ, we both have equal and direct access in the realm of the Holy Spirit to come before the Father!"*

♥ When Jesus died on the cross, the veil that separated us from the presence of God was torn and because of this there is no longer anything that can withhold us from communing with God any longer. He is now closer than the breath that we breathe.

♥ If Jesus didn't die on the cross, we wouldn't be able to access the Father in this way. We can see in the Old Testament that only priests and kings were mainly visited by God's presence during significant times.

♥ It was sin that separated us from God's presence because He is holy. Sin cannot last in His presence, therefore as sinful beings, we couldn't be in closeness with the Father or we wouldn't be able to survive.

♥ Jesus became the mediator between the Father and man when He died on the cross. It was His death that tore the veil so that we could have direct access to the Kingdom of God anytime that we want it.

♥ Ephesians 2:6 even says that we are seated with Him in the heavenly realms which wouldn't be possible without Jesus.

Ephesians 2:19 (NKJV) *"Now, therefore, you are no longer strangers and foreigners* (as before)*, but fellow citizens with the saints and members of the household of God (having all the rights as family members (TPT)).*

Ephesians 2:20 (NKJV) *"Having been built on the foundation of the apostles and prophets. Jesus Christ Himself being the Chief Cornerstone."*
♥ The Passion Translation describes us being raised up like the perfectly fitted stones of the temple. We can see Jesus as the Chief Cornerstone of the temple that holds everything together. The apostles and prophets are those who have walked and are walking with Jesus and lay down the foundation of the Church. Finally, the Church is continuously being built together as the body of Christ. Therefore, it is very important to walk together in unity as a family.

Psalm 133:1 NKJV *"Behold, how good and pleasant it is for brethren to dwell together in unity."*

Ephesians 4:3-4 TPT *"Be faithful to guard the sweet harmony of the Holy Spirit among you in the bonds of peace, being one body and one spirit, as you were all called into the same glorious hope of divine destiny.*

Ephesians 2:21 TPT *"This entire building* (the Church) *is under construction and is continually growing* (never stops expanding territory in the Spirit) *under His* (Jesus- the Chief Cornerstone) *supervision until it rises up completed as the holy temple of the Lord Himself."*
♥ God is transforming each one of us into His likeness, His own dwelling place through the power of the Holy Spirit living in us. (verse 22)

Holy Spirit

O n the Day of Pentecost read about in Acts 2, the Father sends His own Spirit to come and dwell on the earth. This is so that He could once again walk in perfect union with us and ignite us with power to help us walk out our journey with Him. Since He lives within us, we have constant access to the Kingdom of God and are brought from glory to glory (2 Corinthians 3:18 NIV). This is with the purpose of being transformed to look more like Him until He is able to *"present her to himself as a radiant church, without stain or wrinkle or any other blemish, but holy and blameless"* **Ephesians 5:27 NIV.**

♥ With the Spirit of God dwelling within us, we have access to His presence at all times. This includes the moments that we need joy, peace, a comforter, a guide, a teacher, someone to help us in times of need, defender, protector, best friend, etc.

Ephesians 3:16 TPT *"I pray He would unveil within you the unlimited riches of His glory and favour until supernatural strength floods your innermost being with His divine might and explosive power. Then, by constantly using your faith, the life of Christ will be released inside you and the resting place of His love will become the very source and root of your life"*

John 14:15-17 TPT *"Loving Me empowers you to do My commands. And I will ask the Father and He will give you another Helper, the Holy Spirit of Truth, who will be to you a friend just like me- and He will never leave or forsake you. The world cannot receive Him because they do not know Him. But you will know him* *intimately, because He will make His home in you and will live inside you."*

♥   God lives in us to help us

Read **Acts 2:1-13**

♥   The day of Pentecost was a fulfillment of Jesus' word when He said to His disciples that He would send them another Helper.

John 14:18-20 TPT *"I promise that I will never leave you helpless or abandon you as orphans- I will come back to you! Soon I will leave this world and they will see me no longer, but you will see me, because I will live again, and you will come alive too. So when that day comes, you will know that I am living in the Father and that you are one with me, for I will be living in you."*

John 14:23 TPT *"Jesus replied "Loving Me empowers you to obey My word and My Father will love you so deeply that we will come to you and make you our dwelling place"*

♥   Love for Christ is proven and demonstrated by our obedience to all He says.

♥   Interesting how *He* comes to *us*. We can see that it's not by our own efforts but by His grace and kindness towards us. He seeks us out because He desires our hearts. Draw near to God and He will draw near to you.

John 14:26 TPT *"But when the Father sends the Spirit of Holiness, the One like me who sets you free, He will teach you ALL things in My name. And He will inspire you to remember every word that I've told you."*

John 14: 27 TPT *"I leave the gift of peace with you- my peace. Not the kind of fragile peace given by the world, but my perfect peace. Don't yield to fear or be troubled in your hearts- instead be courageous!"*

The Father

It is the Father in which all things consist and have its being. He is the creator and sustainer of all things. He knows the end from the beginning and is the Judge of the whole world. Both Jesus and Holy Spirit respond to God, as the Word says that Jesus only does what He sees the Father doing. Holy Spirit is the Father's own spirit living and dwelling within us. We were created to live in friendship with the Father and when we pass away, we will return to the Father!

In John 15: 1-7 we see God as the Vinedresser, Jesus as the Living Vine and His children as the branches.
He takes up to Himself every fruitless branch to enhance their growth, to prune and to cleanse.

1 John 2:23 TPT *"Whoever rejects the Son, rejects the Father. Whoever embraces the Son, embraces the Father also."*

♥   Jesus is in the Father, the Father is in the Son and they are united as one. When we look upon the nature and character of Jesus, we see the exact likeness of the Father because they are one. To know the nature of Jesus is to know the nature of the Father

♥   Some of His characteristics include kindness, gentleness, faithfulness, patience, merciful, etc.

John 14:9 TPT *"Anyone who has looked at Me has seen the Father. Don't you believe that the Father is living in Me and I am living in the Father?"*

♥   This applies to us as sons and daughters since we are all one, designed to be unified with Jesus and each other. In Ephesians 4:4 we see that we are found in Jesus just as Jesus is found in the Father, therefore, we too are found in the Father.

♥   Jesus only ever did just as the Father told Him to do, He lived in close communion and conversation with God all the time.

♥   We can walk just as Jesus did, in 24/7 communion with God.

God is the Righteous Judge and Jesus is the High Priest, therefore we will all give account to God at the end of our lives, believers and unbelievers.
God is the Judge over sin, man is not. Yet, on earth we still experience natural consequences for sin, but we will also give an eternal account to God. (Read Romans 2)

Romans 2:4 TPT *"Do you not realize that all the wealth of His extravagant kindness is meant to melt your heart and lead you into repentance?"*

♥   He is merciful, righteous and He judges rightly.

♥   When we experience the kindness of the Father, naturally we will be led into repentance for our sins.

Romans 8:31 NKJV *"If God is for us, who could be against us?"*

♥   God is our Defender and this makes us victorious in His name. He fights on our behalf even when we don't see it.

♥   Read about the security we have in God in Psalm 91

Romans 8:32 TPT *"For God has proved His love by giving us His greatest treasure, the gift of His Son. And since God freely offered him up as the sacrifice* *for us all, he certainly won't withhold from us anything else he has to give."*

♥　He bankrupted Heaven so that we could be saved and experience eternal bliss with God in heaven and on earth.

♥　If He was willing to sacrifice His own son for our sake, there is nothing we ask Him for that He would withhold from us when it is in alignment with His will for our lives.

♥　He is not a God that withholds from His kids, He always gives good gifts and works everything together for our good and His glory. (Romans 8:28)

Romans 8:33 TPT *"Who then would dare accuse those whom God has chosen in love to be His? God Himself is the Judge who has issued His final verdict over them- not guilty!"*

Romans 8:34 TPT *"Who then is left to condemn us? Certainly not Jesus, the Anointed One! For He gave His own life for us and conquered death and is now risen, exalted and enthroned at God's right hand. So how could He possibly condemn us since He is continually praying for our triumph?"*

♥　Not only does Holy Spirit intercede for us, so does Jesus! Two divine intercessors are praying for you each day. Two thirds of the Trinity are actively engaged in intercession for us at every moment.

God's love is demonstrated in **Romans 8:35-37** that says: *"Who shall separate us from the love of Christ? Shall tribulation, or distress, or persecution, or famine, or nakedness, or peril, or sword? As it is written: "For Your sake we are killed all day long; We are accounted as sheep for the slaughter." Yet in all these things we are more than conquerors through Him who* *loved us. For I am persuaded that neither death nor life, nor angels nor principalities nor powers, nor things present nor things to come, not height nor depth, nor any other created thing, shall be able to separate us from the love of God which is in Christ Jesus our Lord."*

STORY TIME

When I was sixteen years old, I decided to spend the entire summer at a summer camp as a cabin counsellor. I remember about half-way through my stay there, I was having a very hard day since in my teenage years I dealt with anxiety and always felt the need to strive and perform in order to be loved and accepted by others. At the end of the day, I went to my room to pray and process with the Lord and the moment that I sat on my bed, I began to cry. *"Lord,"* I asked, *"why is life so hard? Why do I always feel so alone and worthless? I know that You love me, but I feel like there is no reason that You should. Please give me a reason, I need to know."*

In that moment, I could feel the sweet presence of the Holy Spirit fill my dorm room as I began to see a vision from the Lord. I am a little girl again, walking somewhere all by myself, with no one to hold my hand or comfort me. Suddenly, looking up I can see a hand extending towards me and as I reach up to take it I know that I am safe with this Person. Hand in hand walking together, I hear a voice say so gently to me *"Because I am your Father."* This was such a redemptive thing to hear that the rest of the night I wept, as I felt the near embrace of the Father through the Holy Spirit. Growing up without a father by my side, and always feeling alone, this encounter with Abba's love has healed my heart in a way that has forever changed me. If anyone desires to know and encounter Him as the Father, ask Him and He will show you.

PRAY WITH ME:

Dear Heavenly Father,

Thank you for choosing us before the foundation of the world so that you might know us and walk in communion with us. Thank you for sending our Lord Jesus Christ to die on the cross for our sins that we should be made holy and blameless before you in love. Thank you that you have predestined us to be adopted as sons by Jesus Christ to Yourself according to the good pleasure of your will, to the praise and glory of your grace.

Thank you for sending Your Holy Spirit on the Day of Pentecost to fill us so that we can walk in the fullness of the Gospel. Thank you for the wisdom and revelation that You impart to us and that by the Holy Spirit you have given us not the spirit of fear, but of power, love and a sound mind.

I pray that you would enlighten the eyes of our understanding and help us to know the love of Christ which passes knowledge, that we may be filled with all the fullness of God.

In Jesus' name,

Amen

PERSONAL APPLICATION QUESTIONS

What is the purpose of Holy Spirit living within us?

_____

_____

_____

_____

_____

_____

Why was the veil torn after Jesus died on the cross?

_____

_____

_____

_____

_____

_____

Why is it important that we walk in unity with one another?

_____

_____

_____

_____

_____

_____

Who is God transforming us to look more alike every day?

_____

_____

_____

_____

_____

_____

_____

DEVOTIONAL 2
PLANTED: THE ESSENTIAL GOSPEL

This devotional is designed to explain the Gospel in a bullet point format so that it is easy to follow and understand. From the beginning of time when God created the heavens and the earth, to the coming of the Holy Spirit on the Day of Pentecost, until now and forever, the Gospel story is what brings freedom and light to every individual who receives it as truth. I will conclude this devotional with a personal testimony and a prayer to follow, as well as a personal application activity.

STARTING FROM THE BEGINNING

♥   God created the whole world in six days and rested on the seventh. He observed it and called it "good". He was pleased with all that He had made.

♥   On the 6th day He created Adam and Eve, called it "very good" and loved them deeply.

♥   He walked with them in the garden, gave them dominion over all He had made and even allowed Adam to name all of His precious animals.

♥   The only thing that they were forbidden to touch was the Tree of the Knowledge of Good and Evil. They were not to eat the fruit of that tree for it would cause darkness to enter the world.

♥   One day, the enemy of our souls went to Eve and deceived her. He lied to her and seduced her into believing that God was a liar and was withholding good things from her by not allowing her to eat from the tree.

♥ **Psalm 84:11 NKJV** *"No good thing will He withhold from those who walk uprightly."*

♥ She ate the fruit and gave some to Adam.

♥ Sin came into the world and because of this they could no longer walk with God in the Garden. They became covered in guilt and shame, afraid of the perfect and loving God who had stitched them together.

♥ God is sinless, all glorious and filled with light, no darkness abides in Him. Neither can darkness abide *with* Him. Light and darkness cannot dwell together, because darkness cannot exist in the presence of light.

♥ **John 1:5 NIV** *"The light shines in the darkness, and the darkness has not overcome it."*

♥ Therefore, man could no longer be in God's presence or they would literally be consumed by the glory of God. The earth would be swallowed up because darkness cannot last a second in the presence of God.

♥ So, we needed a Saviour

♥ This was God's heart as He longed to restore us back to the design that He had intended for us from the very beginning: to be in constant communion with God and live in eternal bliss. God loves to restore us and give us abundant life!

♥ So, He promised to fix what they had done by sending His Son to save all of mankind.

♥ Years later, in humility and the likeness of man God Himself entered into the world as a newborn baby named Jesus. Born into a lowly family and of a virgin, Jewish woman named Mary.

♥ Almost all of mankind was expecting the Saviour of the world to show up as an authoritative and demanding King, instead of as a baby. Therefore the Jewish people did not believe that their Saviour had come.

♥ Jesus grew into a man and faced mundane life with all of its hardships, just like the rest of humanity. He was tempted, tried and rejected.

♥ Jesus was about thirty years of age when His ministry began after He was baptized by His cousin, John the Baptist. After His baptism, the heavens opened up & the Father declares over Jesus *"This is My beloved Son, in whom I am well pleased"* **(Mathew 3:17)**

♥ It is the same with us since we are God's beloved children just as much as Jesus is. We need to do nothing in order to prove ourselves to earn God's love. He was pleased with Jesus before His ministry even began.

♥ **Ephesians 2:8 TPT** *"For by grace you have been saved by faith. Nothing you did could ever earn this salvation, for it was the love gift from God that brought us to Christ! So no one will ever be able to boast, for salvation is never a reward for good works or human striving."*

♥ He walked the earth alongside His 12 disciples, loving them deeply, teaching them in the Fathers way, correcting them, embracing them and guiding them. At the same time, He was also destroying every old way of thinking and breaking off the bondage of religion and law that they had always lived under. They experienced the Kingdom of God and fell in love with the Father as they witnessed His own character shining through His Son Jesus. He taught them to pray & demonstrated the power of God through healings and wonders. He taught them 24/7 communion with the Father through His day-to-day lifestyle. He flipped everything they had believed about God, upside down. They began to see God as an ever-present, loving saviour and friend to them rather than a distant, stoic man of condemnation and judgement.

♥   Even Jesus was tempted by the devil, yet He overcame by the power of His testimony which is the Word of God.

♥   He was rejected and wounded by man, but never retaliated or insulted in return. He kept silent for He knew that the Lord's will was good. He had a plan to demolish death and bring the Kingdom to earth. Jesus trusted His Father and endured the momentary suffering for the sake of the world.

♥   **1 Peter 2:23 NIV** *"When they hurled insults at Him, He did not retaliate; when He suffered He made no threats. Instead, He entrusted Himself to Him who judges justly."*

♥   He knew all of our suffering and bore the weight of sin on the cross. He is a God who comes close in suffering and brokenness, comforting all those who mourn because He too knows great pain.

♥   **Psalm 34:18 NIV** *"The Lord is close to the broken-hearted and comforts all who are crushed in spirit"*

♥   When the assigned time had come, He permitted the Roman soldiers to arrest Him.

♥   Prior to this moment, Jesus had spent the hours before His arrest in the Garden of Gethsemane where He cried out to God in deep intercession, to the point of bleeding from His face. The time had come for Him to give His life and as the weight of the world laid upon Him it crushed Him. The enemy was trying to take His life through this deep pain. In desperation, He cried out *"Lord, take this cup of suffering from me"* He asked the Father to remove this cup from Him so that He would not prematurely die from its weight before He could surrender His life on the cross for the sake of the world. He needed to give up His life willingly, not have it stolen.

♥   Nobody could take His life, but He gave it freely and allowed Himself to suffer so that mankind could be made whole by the power of His blood.

♥   **John 10:18 NIV** *"No one takes it from me, but I lay it down of my own accord. I have authority to lay it down and authority to take it up again. This command I received from my Father."*

♥   After the Roman soldiers arrested Jesus, they handed Him over to the authorities where He would later be spit on and whipped 39 times by spiked tools until His bones could be seen through His skin.

♥   **Isaiah 53:5 NKJV** *"But He was wounded for our transgressions; He was bruised for our iniquities; The chastisement for our peace was upon Him, And by His stripes we are healed."*

♥   A crown of thorns was later pushed into His scalp and He was commanded by the authorities to carry His heavy cross to the location that He would be crucified. There He would be nailed to the cross by His hands and feet and after hours of hanging on it in the blistering sun, they would pierce Him in the side with a spear and watch His blood pour out.

♥   He chose this path to redeem what had been stolen in the garden and to give us freedom from the chains of sin and death.

♥   **Luke 23:34 NKJV** describes His mercy when right before He breathed His last breath, He still cried out *"Father, forgive them for they know not what they do."* (On the day of Pentecost, the same city that crucified Jesus radically encountered the love of God and received salvation. **Acts 2**)

♥   The moment He died, the veil that separated the holy place from the inner holy of holies found inside of the tent of meeting was torn. This represented that the divide between God's presence and man was removed and He could once again come close to His children.

♥ He was desperate to dwell among His children again. Light had surely overcome. Death, where is your sting? **(1 Corinthians 15:55-57)**

♥ Jesus then went down to the grave for three days and took back the keys to death and Hades that is described in **Revelation 1:18 NIV** where He proclaims *"I am the Living One; I was dead, and now look, I am alive for ever and ever! And I hold the keys of death and Hades."*

♥ Therefore, the devil has no more power leaving us to be victorious in Christ for all of eternity since Jesus has won the war! He emptied the grave and literally faced death so that He could conquer it forever.

♥ After three days, Jesus was resurrected from the grave. The stone was rolled away from the tomb where He was laid, and it was found empty. **(Luke 24:2)**

♥ He walked with the disciples for 40 days before He ascended to Heaven to be with the Father. During this time He proclaimed eternal salvation to the disciples and called them into the "Great Commission". **(Mathew 28:16-20)**

♥ **John 16:7 NKJV** *"Nevertheless, I tell you the truth: it is to your advantage that I go away, for if I do not go away, the Helper will not come to you. But if I depart, I will send Him to you."* Jesus had to leave so that the Holy Spirit could come.

♥ This was the reason that He gave up His life on the cross: so that we could have 24/7 access to the Kingdom of God living within us; to dwell in Him and He in us; and so that He would no longer be separated from His kids and His presence would be able to dwell on the earth in fullness.

♥   Then on the Day of Pentecost, as the disciples were all gathered together in one place. *"Suddenly there came a sound from heaven, as of a rushing mighty wind, and it filled the whole house where they were sitting. Then there appeared to them divided tongues, as of fire, and one sat upon each of them. And they were all filled with the Holy Spirit and began to speak with other tongues, as the Spirit gave them utterance"* **(Acts 2:1-4 NKJV)**

♥   It was Holy Spirit that gave the apostles the power to preach the word and perform the miracles of God. It is this same Spirit that we all have access to today and because of Him, we can experience the fullness of the Gospel in all of its power.

♥   In **Mathew 3:11 NKJV** John the Baptist speaks of the coming of Jesus when he states that *"I indeed baptize you with water unto repentance, but He who is coming after me is mightier than I, whose sandals I am not worthy to carry. **He will baptize you with the Holy Spirit and fire.**"* I encourage you to ask for this baptism unto fire.

STORY TIME

I was saved when I was 12 years old after I started attending a church with my friend from school every weekend. Growing up life was difficult, and I never really experienced the joy that I saw that the people at church had. I knew that they carried something that I did not and my curiosity of what this could be kept me attending every week. For about two years I continued going to church, youth groups, and even summer camp regularly. I began to learn so much about God from my peers and leaders, however I was still struggling endlessly with addiction to pornography, anxiety, depression and the stored-up anger inside of my heart. I loved being at church because life felt easy within its walls, but the very moment that I stepped outside, the reality of my broken life and family would hit me like a truck. It wasn't until I was fourteen years old that I experienced the power of the Holy Spirit which changed everything for me.

I was with a group of my "crazy Christian" friends who pulled me along on an activity called a "treasure hunt" where we would ask the Holy Spirit for clues about who to pray for in our community. This was a strange concept for me, but again my curiosity and hunger for more of God led me to participate. Eventually, my team ended up at Superstore on the search for a man with an injury. While we were still in the parking lot, a friend of mine approached me and asked if I had ever been filled with the Holy Spirit or spoken in tongues as described in 1 Corinthians 14:2. Of course, this was foreign and slightly disturbing to me, so I said no. But as he further described to me the power and freedom that it brings to a believer's life, I couldn't help but be hungry for it. If there was any chance that this was the missing part of my life, I figured it couldn't hurt to ask him if he would pray for me to receive this gift. With my hands held out in front of me and a quick prayer from my friends, I could feel a gentle wind surrounding me and electricity beginning to run through my bones. It was in that moment in the parking lot of Superstore that everything changed for me as I began to speak in a foreign language and encounter God in a way that I had never experienced before.

Immediately after, we went inside to pray over a man who would encounter Jesus and receive the love of God for the first time. I knew in my heart that I was changed from the inside out and that it was this baptism of the Holy Spirit that I was missing for so long. After this moment everything began to shift in my life, from the addictions I had, to my relationships, insecurities and radical healing over mental trauma. I encourage you friends, if you are hungry for a greater encounter with God and to be filled with His own Spirit in a greater measure, begin to cry out to God and He will give it to you.

"Where, O death, is your victory?
Where, O death, is your sting?
The sting of death is sin, and the power of sin is the law. But thanks be to God! He gives us the victory through our Lord Jesus Christ."
(1 Corinthians 15:55-57 NIV)

PRAY WITH ME:

Dear Heavenly Father,

I come to You in the Name of Jesus.

*Your Word says that "anyone who calls on the name of the Lord shall be saved" **(Acts 2:21)** Jesus I ask that You come into my heart and be the Lord over my life as I believe that You were raised from the dead. (Romans 10:9-10) I also ask that you fill me with the Holy Spirit and baptize me in fire as You give me utterance. (Acts 2:4, 1 Corinthians 14:2)*

Thank you that I am perfectly loved by You and that I am saved by Your grace.

In Jesus Name,

Amen

APPLY IT TO PRACTICE IT

Grab a buddy and practice preaching the Gospel to one another as if it's their first time ever hearing it!

DEVOTIONAL 3
PLANTED: JESUS' CALL TO FOLLOW

This devotion examines the cost of following Jesus and being obedient to the call of God on our lives. Even though the call may be costly, it is worth it. I will differentiate between reward and salvation as well as give a personal example of how God called me to follow Him and surrender everything to follow His lead.

Mathew 16:24 TPT *"Then Jesus said to His disciples, "If you truly want to follow Me, you should at once completely reject and disown your own life. And you must be willing to share my cross and experience it as your own, as you continually surrender to My ways. For if you choose self- sacrifice and lose your lives for my glory, you will continually discover true life. But if you choose to keep your lives for yourselves, your will forfeit what you try to keep. For even if you were to gain all the wealth and power of this world with everything it could offer you- at the cost of your own life- what good would that be? And what could be more valuable to you than your own soul?"*

- ♥ This same passage spoke by Jesus is also found in Mark 8:34, Luke 9:23

John 14:6 NKJV *"Jesus said to him, "I am the way and the truth and the life. No one comes to the Father except through me."*

- ♥ We must know Jesus intimately.
- ♥ *"Not everyone who says to Me, 'Lord, Lord,' shall enter the kingdom of Heaven, but He who does the will of My Father in Heaven. Many will*

say to Me in that day, 'Lord, Lord, have we not prophesied in Your name, cast out demons in Your name, and done many wonders in your name?' And then I will declare to them, 'I never knew you; depart from Me, you who practice lawlessness!' **(Mathew 7:21-23 NKJV)**

♥ To follow Him is more than what we **do** for God. We are called to know Him personally by sitting at His feet and seeking His face.

♥ **Mathew 6:33 NIV** *"Seek first the Kingdom of God and all these things will be given to you as well."*

♥ It's not about what you accomplish for God but about what He accomplishes through you as you yield everything to Him and learn to hear His voice in the secret place. We are called to REST in His love, not perform. As we seek Him, He helps us to walk right into our destiny- this is nothing that we can accomplish on our own strength

♥ **John 10:27 NKJV** *"My sheep hear my voice, and I know them, and they follow me"*

♥ We learn the Father's voice by sitting in His presence and spending time in His word.

Many of times in the gospels, Jesus emphasizes that following Him means surrendering everything to Him and walking away from our old ways of life. When we lose ourselves, we gain the Kingdom of God.

Read **Mathew 19:16-30** of the rich young man that questions Jesus

♥ In order to truly follow Jesus, we must be willing to surrender everything at His feet. We cannot serve two masters. Our first love must be Jesus alone as we cannot serve our earthly pleasures and Jesus at the same time.

Romans 8:7-10 TPT *"In fact, the mind-set focused on the flesh fights God's plan and refuses to submit to His direction, because it cannot! For no matter how hard they try, God finds no pleasure with those who are controlled by the flesh. But when the Spirit of Christ empowers your life, you are not dominated by the flesh but by the Spirit. And if you are not joined to the Spirit of the Anointed One, you are not of Him. Now Christ lives His life in you! And even though your body may be dead because of the effects of sin, His life-giving Spirit imparts life to you because you are fully accepted by God."*

Romans 8:12-13 TPT *"So then, beloved ones, the flesh has no claims on us at all and we have no further obligation to live in obedience to it. For when you live controlled by the flesh, you are about to die. But if the life of the Spirit puts to death the corrupt ways of the flesh, we then taste his abundant life."*

♥ We are called to walk in submission to the Spirit of God, doing what is pleasing to the Father. If we submit to our flesh, we are slaves to the flesh and its sinful nature. If we submit to God, we can walk in full freedom.

♥ *"Where the Spirit of the Lord is, there is freedom."* **(2 Corinthians 3:17)**

1 John 2:15-17 NKJV *"Do not love the world or anything in the world. If anyone loves the world, love for the Father is not in them. For everything in the world—the lust of the flesh, the lust of the eyes, and the pride of life—comes not from the Father but from*

the world. The world and its desires pass away, but whoever does the will of God lives forever."
- None of our earthly pleasures will be carried with us beyond this life, so why do we store up for ourselves earthly treasures and experiences that are of no eternal value? **(Mathew 6:19-21)**

"As a prisoner of the Lord, I plead you to walk holy, in a way that is suitable to your high rank, given to you in your divine calling." **(Ephesians 4:1 TPT)**
- We cannot walk worthy of our call during this lifetime if we do not walk closely alongside the Father.
- As we gaze upon the Father, we become like the Father and are transformed into His likeness from glory to glory. **(2 Corinthians 3:18)**
- We become what we behold.

Romans 14:12 NKJV *"So then, each of us will give an account of ourselves to God."*

2 Corinthians 5:10 NKJV *'For we must all appear before the judgement seat of Christ, that each one may receive the things done in the body, according to what he has done, whether good or bad.'*

- As individuals we will all give an account for our lives in Heaven. I want my entire life to have been pleasing to God. This comes from intimacy with God. Remember that when Jesus was baptized, the Father declared over Him that he was 'well pleased' **(Mathew 3:17)** before His ministry even truly started, because He walked very closely alongside His Father.

Reward VS. Salvation.
It is abundantly clear from Scripture that we cannot earn our salvation. It is God's gift of grace to us when we receive Christ as our Saviour.

"Not by works of righteousness which we have done, but according to His mercy He saved us, through the washing of regeneration and renewing of the Holy Spirit." **Titus 3:5 NKJV**

♥ However, once we receive Christ as our Savior we have the ability to earn eternal reward as we walk in obedience to the call of God on our lives. The believer receives these rewards at the judgement seat of Christ when we come before Him on Judgement Day.

The Apostle Paul describes it like this: *"For no-one can lay any foundation other than the one already laid, which is Jesus Christ. If anyone builds on this foundation using gold, silver, costly stones, wood, hay or star, their work will be shown for what it is, because the Day will bring it to light. It will be revealed with fire, and the fire will test the quality of each man's work. If what he has built survives, the builder will receive a reward. If it is burned up, the builder will suffer loss but yet will be saved- even though only as one escaping through the flames."* **(1 Corinthians 3:11-15 NIV)**

♥ Therefore, at the judgement seat of Christ we will receive reward for our obedience to God's word.
♥ Although no amount of works can earn us salvation, acceptance, or love from God, good

works do lead those who have loved Christ in faithful service to receive reward in Heaven.

Romans 10: 9 NKJV *"If you confess with your mouth the Lord Jesus and believe in your heart that God has raised him from the dead, you will be saved."*

- ♥ Therefore, if you confess with your mouth that Jesus is Lord, you will be saved and have eternal life. BUT what you do with your life matters. The Word says that if your works were of wood, hay and straw- they will burn up before you and you will face the loss of the rewards that you could have had upon your arrival in heaven.
- ♥ We have total access to the kingdom of God NOW by the Spirit of God. Why not make use of the life He paid for us to have on the cross?

John 15:4-11 TPT *"So you must remain in life- union with me, for I remain in life-union with you. For as a branch is severed from the vine will not bear fruit, so your life will be fruitless unless you live your life intimately joined to mine. I am the sprouting vine and you're my branches. As you live in union with me as your source, fruitfulness will stream from within you- but when you live separated from Me you are powerless. If a person is separated from Me, he is discarded; such branches are gathered up and thrown into the fire to be burned. But if you live in life-union with me and if my words live powerfully within you- then you can ask whatever you desire and it will be done. When your lives bear abundant fruit, you demonstrate that you are my mature disciples who glorify my Father! I love each of you with the same love that the Father loves Me. You must continually* *let my love nourish your hearts. If you keep My commands, you will live in my love, just as I have kept my Father's commands, for I continually live nourished and empowered by His love. My purpose for telling you these things is so that the joy that I experience will fill your hearts with overflowing gladness!"*

- ♥ To follow God and experience all that He has in store for us, requires us to abide and remain in Him. You cannot bear fruit if you do not abide in Him and His word. In fact, this passage tells us that if we live separated from God, we will be discarded and powerless. If we live in communion with Him, we can ask for anything in His name and it will be done for us! We will live in the power of the Spirit and be fruitful, empowered and nourished by His love!

Song of Solomon 8:7 TPT *"Rivers of pain and persecution will never extinguish this flame. Endless floods will be unable to quench this raging fire that burns within you. Everything will be consumed. It will stop at nothing as you yield everything to this furious fire **until it won't even seem to you like a sacrifice anymore."***

- ♥ When we think about what Jesus did for us on the cross and that we now get to experience the Kingdom of God on earth and in Heaven for all eternity…there is truly nothing that could compare to His sacrifice for us. It is an HONOR to give up our lives for the Gospel, since He gave everything up for us.
- ♥ As we yield everything in our lives to Him and continue to grow in relationship with the Father,

our love will become so strong that following God won't seem like a sacrifice, but instead a joy and a privilege.

♥ Jesus was in 24/7 communion with God therefore dying on the cross was a privilege rather than a burden. This is because He knew His Father's nature and that He could be fully trusted. Jesus' trust in the Father led Him to be totally yielded to His ways, no matter what.

Holy Spirit is our Helper, (John 14:26) ask Him and He will help you live for God.

♥ Just like in Song of Solomon 8, Jesus' love desires to consume everything in you that is not of Him, including unforgiveness, trauma, addiction, depression, anxiety, etc. This happens by remaining and abiding in Him and His Word. Our greatest victories should happen in the secret place with God. As you begin to have a better understanding of His deep and unwavering love for you, it will seem like less of a sacrifice to yield your life to Him.

1 Peter 2:9 TPT *"But you are God's chosen treasure-priests who are kings, a spiritual "nation" set apart as God's devoted ones. He called you out of darkness to experience His marvelous light, and now He claims you as His very own. He did this so that you would broadcast His glorious wonders throughout the world."*

♥ Therefore, let's walk worthy of your divine call!

Romans 8:15 NLT *"So you have not received a spirit that makes you fearful slaves. Instead, you received God's Spirit when he adopted you as his own children. Now we call him, "Abba, Father."*

- ♥ It's so important that we know who we are as sons and daughters of God.
- ♥ He has adopted us as His own children and are not His slaves, but rather his children whom he adores and gave His own son for. We do not serve Him out of obligation, but because we love Him since it is a relationship and not a religion.

John 3:16 NIV *"For God so loved the world that He gave His one and only Son, that whoever believes in him shall not perish but have eternal life."*

STORY TIME

When I was nineteen, I was working a fulltime desk job, had an awesome friend group, drove an expensive car, and all around loved my comfortable life. But one day God asked me to leave it all behind and move to a ranch in the middle of nowhere with no cell service, and A LOT of snow keeping me stranded there most days. I knew that I was being called by God to separate myself for a year to seek Him without distraction and to find the healing that I needed from my past. At the time the cost of this felt very big because of all that I would leave behind. I knew that this decision would change the relationships I had with my friends, take away the security of my job, and be an all-around challenging experience. One morning I was expressing to God my concern about all that I would lose in saying yes to Him and He led me to the passage above in **Mathew 16:24-26 TPT** where Jesus says to His disciples:

"If you truly want to follow Me, you should at once completely reject and disown your own life. And you must be willing to share my cross and experience it as your own, as you continually surrender to My ways. For if you choose self- sacrifice and lose your lives for my glory, you will continually discover true life. But if you choose to keep your lives for yourselves, your will forfeit what you try to keep. For even if you were to gain all the wealth and power of this world with everything it could offer you- at the cost of your own life- what good would that be? And what could be more valuable to you than your own soul?"

He showed me through this that everything I try to keep, I will lose anyways if I deny the call of God on my life. I could have chosen to say no to God and try to keep life the way that it was, but the reality is that everything would have changed anyways and I would have been entirely disobedient to the Lord, wishing that I hadn't been. Interestingly, a few months into living at this Ranch, the friend group I spent time with entirely changed, my car was totaled in an accident and the Lord provided all that I needed during my stay there. God's call on your life may be costly, but it is worth it. The year of time away that I gave to the Lord altered my life forever and prepared me for all that I am walking in right now. I wouldn't give that time away for anything!

"Never doubt God's mighty power to work in you and accomplish all this. He will achieve infinitely more than your greatest request, your most unbelievable dream, and exceed your wildest imagination! He will outdo them all, for his miraculous power constantly energizes you."
Ephesians 3:20 TPT

PRAY WITH ME:

Dear Heavenly Father,

Thank you that the call to follow you may be costly, but it is worth it. You are worth my life laid down. I ask that you'd consume everything within me that is hindering me from following Your voice. Help me to yield to Your love as I grow in you each day, and that I would recognize that following You isn't a sacrifice considering all that you did for me on the cross. Help me to lose myself in You, so that I can gain the Kingdom.

In Jesus name,

Amen

PERSONAL APPLICATION QUESTIONS

What does it look like to surrender your life fully to the Lord?

_____

_____

_____

_____

_____

_____

_____

Is there anything God is asking you to lay down to help you in serving Him better?

_____

_____

_____

_____

_____

_____

_____

Are you willing to obey His voice no matter what the cost? Why?

_____

_____

_____

_____

_____

_____

_____

DEVOTIONAL 4
PLANTED: SUPREME COMMAND OF LOVE

This devotion gives insight into loving God and loving others. When we truly love God and experience His love for us every-day, we are empowered to love others better and to *"love because He first Loved us."* (1 John 4:19) I will conclude with a personal testimony, followed by a prayer, and some personal application questions.

Mark 12:30-31 NKJV *"And you shall love the Lord your God with all your heart and with all your soul and with all your mind and with all your strength.' This is the first commandment. And the second, like it, is this: 'You shall love your neighbour as yourself.' There is no commandment greater than these."*

Mathew 22:36-40 NKJV *""Teacher, which is the greatest commandment in the Law?"*
Jesus said to him, '"You shall love the Lord your God with all your heart and with all your soul and with all your mind.' This is the first and great commandment. And the second is like it: 'Love your neighbour as yourself.'"

- ♥ When we love God, we can't help but to love others, as well as who God created us to be. Loving others and our-selves go hand in hand.
- ♥ Love is our highest calling- everything that we do should be done in love and in knowing that it is out of our love for God that we serve Him. Not as a slave, but as an adopted and accepted son or daughter.

Read **Romans 8:31-39**

- ❤ Nothing can separate us from His love and because of this we can rest knowing that we cannot earn God's approval. When we know that we are loved deeply & unconditionally-then we are free to love others out of this place.

Romans 2:6 NKJV *"God will render to each one according to his deeds."*
- ❤ It is not our job as Christians to extend judgement toward others, it is God's since He is the righteous Judge.
- ❤ It is our job to only love the world and lead it to Jesus through the way that we live and love.

Romans 14:12 NKJV *"So then, each one of us will give an account of ourselves to God"*
- ❤ We do not give an account to the Lord for anyone but ourselves, therefore; we do not need to condemn or judge others by the way they are living, even if they offend us. Take responsibility for the way that you respond and aim to be reflective of the Lord's merciful nature.
- ❤ Let's take responsibility for our actions and words alone since we cannot make other people's actions our responsibility. Allow the Lord deal with them rightfully.

Mathew 5:44 NIV *"But I tell you, love your enemies and pray for those who persecute you!"*
- ❤ It is not our job to take revenge, to convince others of their wrongdoings, or to convict others of sin. It is our job to LOVE.

- ♥ Pray for those who are in the wrong, do not curse them.
- ♥ **Mathew 7:5** Check yourself before you blame others as we can all easily fall into sin. Have grace towards those who are acting out of an orphan spirit!

Romans 3:23 NIV *'For all have sinned and fall short of the glory of God'*

- ♥ Something to remember is that if people really knew who they were, they wouldn't act in a poor manner towards you or others. If WE really knew who we were we wouldn't respond to hurtful behavior in a negative way.

1 Corinthians 13:1-3 TPT *"If I were to speak with eloquence in earth's many languages, and in the heavenly tongues of angels, yet I didn't express myself with love, my words would be reduced to the hollow sound of nothing more than a clanging cymbal. And if I were to have the gift of prophecy with a profound understanding of God's hidden secrets, and if I possessed unending supernatural knowledge, and if I had the greatest gift of faith that could move mountains, but have never learned to love, then I am nothing. And if I were to be so generous as to give away every-thing I owned to feed the poor, and to offer my body to be burned as a martyr, without the pure motive of love, I would have gained nothing of value."*

- ♥ Love needs to be the hidden intention of every good work, otherwise it will count for nothing in Heaven.

1 Corinthians 13:13 TPT *"Until then, there are three things that remain: faith, hope, and love- yet love surpasses them all. So above all else, let love be the beautiful prize for which you run."*

- ♥ Love is greater than all other things, even faith and hope. It is the only one of those three things that is eternal because faith and hope is what we live by on earth to help us continue pressing on toward Heaven.
- ♥ **Verses 8-10** *"Love never stops loving. It extends beyond the gift of prophecy, which eventually fades away. It is more enduring than tongues, which will one day fall silent. Love remains long after words of knowledge are forgotten. Our present knowledge and our prophecies are but partial, but when love's perfection arrives, the partial will fade away."*

John 13:35 NIV *"By this everyone will know that you are my disciples, if you love one another"*

- ♥ We testify the gospel to the world and show that we are Christians by our LOVE.

1 Corinthians 13: 4-8 TPT *"Love is large and incredibly patient. Love is gentle and consistently kind to all. It refuses to be jealous when blessing comes to someone else. Love does not brag about one's achievements nor inflate its own importance. Love does not traffic in shame and disrespect, nor selfishly seek its own honor. Love is not easily irritated or quick to take offence. Love joyfully celebrates honesty and finds no delight in what is wrong. Love is a safe place of shelter, for it never stops believing the best for others. Love never takes failure as defeat, for it never gives up."*

♥   God IS Love. Therefore, God is everything described in the passage above. Since we are sons and daughters of God, we are called to walk in these qualities as well.

Song of Solomon 8:6 TPT *"Fasten me upon your heart as a seal of fire forevermore. This living consuming flame will seal you as my prisoner of love. My passion is stronger than the chains of death and the grave, all-consuming as the very flashes of fire from the burning heart of God."*

- ♥ His love is jealous and passionate. He desires intimacy over everything else and He will pursue our heart until He has it fully. As we pursue Him in friendship, He tends to all of our shortcomings with compassion so that we can go from glory to glory.
- ♥ It's important that we get in the secret place and get to know His love for us. Let's allow everything that is not of Him be taken care of while we are alone in His presence.

John 15:9-17 TPT

- ♥ The Great Commission must be led by love. We want to be a church that leads the world to the Lord through our generous acts of love and through our radical acts of forgiveness. Let us become a broken-hearted generation that cries out for one another from our knees and that bears much fruit by abiding in Jesus.

Ephesians 4:1-2 TPT *"As a prisoner of the Lord, I plead with you to walk holy, in a way that is suitable to your high rank, given to you in your divine calling. With tender humility and quiet patience, always demonstrate gentleness and generous love toward*

one another, especially toward those who may try your patience."
- ♥ It is holy to walk in love as it is walking in alignment with our identity in Christ.

Ephesians 3:17 TPT *"Then, by constantly using your faith, the life of Christ will be released deep inside you, and the resting place of his love will become the very source and root of your life."*
- ♥ We can operate in this overflow everyday by abiding in prayer and the Word of God.

STORY TIME

Growing up, I had a very toxic relationship with my mom. I was angry towards her for so many reasons and circumstances that had occurred in my life and wanted nothing to do with her. There was no trust in our relationship and consistently we would fight as the anger, unforgiveness, and bitterness festered in my heart towards her. Eventually I gave my heart to Jesus and was filled with the Holy Spirit, and later so did she. After much repentance and a regaining of trust I began to see her differently and decided every day that I would choose to love like Jesus instead of walking in hostility towards her. Without the love of Jesus abiding in me, refining my heart and mind, I wouldn't have been able to do that, but because of His love, I was able to forgive and to love her more and more each day. Today we have a great relationship, and I can for sure say that this would not have been possible without God's love first abiding in me.

PRAY WITH ME:

Dear Heavenly Father,

Thank You that You know me and love me perfectly. Thank you that you don't see me for my sin and have already forgiven me on the cross. I want to experience your love in a deeper way. I ask that You teach me how to abide in Your love each day, help me to forgive those who have wronged me and to release any bitterness or unforgiveness to You. Help me to love others like You love me. I love you, Lord.

In Jesus name,

Amen

PERSONAL APPLICATION QUESTIONS

What was God's greatest act of love towards us? Is there a verse that best describes this?

_____
_____
_____
_____
_____
_____

What are some things that God says about His love for you? Do you believe what He says about you?

_____
_____
_____
_____
_____
_____

What are some ways that you can better love the difficult people in your life?

_____
_____
_____
_____
_____
_____

DEVOTIONAL 5
PLANTED: OUR MISSION

G od calls every believer to be a part of the Great Commission. We are all called to preach the Gospel and make disciples of all nations. Below is a brief outline of what this looks like, followed by a testimony, a prayer, and some personal application questions.

Mathew 28:19-20 TPT *"Then Jesus came close to them and said, "All the authority of the universe has been given to me. Now wherever you go, <u>make disciples</u> of all nations, <u>baptizing them in the name of the Father, the Son, and the Holy Spirit</u>. And <u>teach them</u> to faithfully follow all that I have commanded you. And never forget that I am with you every day, even to the completion of this age."*

- ❤ This is a command since it is our primary mission as Christians to partner with God's heart for the world to be saved.
- ❤ This requires obedience, and a "YES" to the call of God on our lives, wherever He is calling us. Whether to our high school and family or across seas... obedience to His voice is required. It's important to remember that we can impact people and make disciples anywhere that we are.

1 Timothy 2:4 NKJV *"who desires that all men to be saved and to come to the knowledge of the truth."*

- ❤ For this to happen, God desires to partner with us in advancing the kingdom of God among the earth.

How to disciple?
- ♥ GO in His authority. Authority comes when we know our identity in Him.
- ♥ Knowing our identity comes by walking closely with the Father and getting in the Word of God.
- ♥ *Preach* the Gospel message by word of mouth.
- ♥ Preach the Gospel through the way that you live and love. Try to demonstrate Jesus to others through your day-to-day lifestyle. Teach them the word and show them how to live it out.
- ♥ They will know us by the fruit that our lives produce when we continue to walk closely with God. It's hard to minister to people when we haven't been filled up by Him first, so it's important to remember that we need to be faithful in spending time with Him in the secret place. Otherwise, we will have nothing to give others.
- ♥ People learn from us and how to serve Jesus by the way that we live, usually not just by the words that we speak.
- ♥ Baptize people in the Father, Son AND the Holy Spirit.
- ♥ Be in the process with people and don't expect them to have it all together and understand everything right away. Remember that there is so much grace in the process.

1 Thessalonians 5:14 NIV *"And we urge you, brothers and sisters, warn those who are idle and disruptive, encourage the disheartened, help the weak, be patient with everyone."*

Romans 12:15 NIV *"Rejoice with those who rejoice; mourn with those who mourn"*
- ♥ Do whatever it takes to minister to people where they are at as the Holy Spirit leads us. It is so important that we do not view ourselves as higher or holier than anyone and to humble ourselves.
- ♥ Aim to learn the culture that is being ministered to.
- ♥ Love people as they are and not how we think they should be.
- ♥ Make FRIENDS, not projects. When we love people, they will learn from our lives.

Mathew 5:13-16 NIV *"You are the salt of the earth. But if the salt loses its saltiness, how can it be made salty again? It is no longer good for anything, except to be thrown out and trampled underfoot. You are the light of the world. A town built on a hill cannot be hidden. Neither do people light a lamp and put it under a bowl. Instead they put it on its stand, and it gives light to everyone in the house. In the same way, let your light shine before others, that they may see your good deeds and glorify your Father in heaven."*

Luke 9:23-26 TPT *Jesus said to all of His followers, "If you truly desire to be my disciple, you must disown your life completely, embrace my 'cross' as your own, and surrender to my ways. For if you choose self-sacrifice, giving up your lives for my glory, you will discover true life. But if you choose to keep your lives for yourselves, you will lose what you try to keep. Even if you gained all the wealth and power of this world, everything it could offer you, yet you lost your soul in the process, what good is that? So why then* *are you ashamed of being my disciple? Are you ashamed of the revelation-truth I give to you?"*

Remember that the Great Commission must be led by love.

STORY TIME

Back in 2018 I travelled to Kona, Hawaii to do a Discipleship Training School at the University of the Nations for 6 months. In this program, we learned all about what it looks like to be a part of the Great Commission, to have boldness in preaching the gospel, as well as how to disciple people of many cultures.

The last two months of the program, we were separated into teams and sent to multiple different countries around the world. My team went to Zambia and Tanzania in Africa. While we were there, we saw thousands of people come to Christ, many healed and set free from physical infirmity and bondage of all kinds. I even saw blind eyes and deaf ears open right in front of me.

One of the major focuses of our team was to spend time encouraging the local churches so that they could continue to disciple believers effectively and further the gospel in their regions. This was very effective and we frequently heard testimonies of lives being transformed as more and more people connected with the local Church community.

Preaching the gospel and discipleship go hand in hand, and it is one of the main responsibilities of the Church to be good stewards of.

PRAY WITH ME:

Dear Heavenly Father,

Thank You that You desire that all should be saved. (1Timothy 2:4) Help me to be a part of the Great Commission to the best of my ability. I ask for Your grace to preach the Gospel and be a bold light in my community, family and places of influence. Help me to be obedient to Your voice and to walk in Your love, extending your love towards others.

In Jesus Name,

Amen

PERSONAL APPLICATION QUESTIONS

Who in your life can you reach out to and show the love of God?

_____

_____

_____

_____

_____

_____

How can you be a greater light in your environment?

_____

_____

_____

_____

_____

_____

Is there a friend(s) in your life that you can walk more closely alongside and pursue God together?

_____

_____

_____

_____

_____

_____

ROOTED

Now that we've been planted in foundational truths, it's time to let our roots go down deep in Him so that we can bear fruit that lasts.

DEVOTIONAL 1
ROOTED: TRANSFORMATION

When God calls us to follow Him, He brings us through a process of transformation. This is so that we can run the race set before us without any sin hindering us or standing between our relationship with God. He desires that we would be holy, set apart and blameless before Him in love and that we would look more and more like Him each day. This devotional touches on the ways that we can grow in this, including a personal testimony, a prayer of consecration and some personal application questions.

Romans 12:2 TPT *"Stop imitating the ideals and opinions of the culture around you but be inwardly transformed by the Holy Spirit through a total reformation of how you think. This will empower you to discern God's will as you live a beautiful life, satisfying and perfect in His eyes."*

What does it look like to be conformed to the world?

Conformed definition: To behave like, to agree with, or to become like.

- ♥ As believers in Christ we are not of this world, but are citizens of His kingdom as **1 Peter 2:11** describes *"As temporary residents and foreigners keep away from worldly desires that wage war against your very souls."*

- ♥ The desires of this world are not of the kingdom of God. They wage war against our souls.
- ♥ **1 John 2:15-17 NKJV** *"Do not love the world or the things in the world. If anyone loves the world, the love of the Father is not in him. For all that is in the world- the lust of the flesh, the lust of the eyes, and the pride of life- is not of the Father but is of the world. And the world is passing away, and the lust of it; but he who does the will of God abides forever."*
- ♥ We are called to live in the same manner as Jesus. He died on the cross so that we can be free from sin, and to share in His kingdom inheritance.
- ♥ When the Pentecost occurred and God send us the Holy Spirit to abide within us, we gained access to all that Jesus has including peace, joy, power, wisdom, abundance, healing, etc.

It doesn't make sense for us to be operating the same way as the world does, for we are sons and daughters of the Almighty God. Do you think that gossip, lying, stealing, fear, anger and sadness occurs in Heaven? Absolutely not!

As children of God, we are now rulers over sin through Jesus's death on the cross, therefore, we can choose to turn from temptation.

- ♥ **Genesis 4:7 NIV** *"But if you do not do what is right, sin is crouching at the door. Its desire is for you, but you must rule over it."*
- ♥ **Ephesians 4:1 NIV** *"As a prisoner for the Lord, then, I urge you to live a life worthy of the calling you have received"*

♥ Example: A princess in a palace would never be cussing and doing drugs while sitting on her throne. She represents her kingdom, and therefore must walk worthy of this role.

John 10:10 NIV *"The thief comes only to steal, kill and destroy; I have come that they may have life, and have it to the full."*
♥ We either serve the Lord or we serve the enemy. When we choose to serve ourselves, we are actually serving the enemy!
♥ Jesus is the only way! His way leads to abundance while the enemy only leads us into destruction.

We need to be transformed by the RENEWAL OF OUR MINDS.
The word 'transformation' implies a dramatic change. It is a metamorphosis; similar to the process a caterpillar goes through when transforming into a butterfly. It becomes a completely new creation!

Renewal defined: To resume after an interruption (sin); to re-establish.

What does it mean to renew your mind?
♥ To clean it up, to fix your perspective, to make new again, to change the pathways.

How do we renew our mind?
♥ By meditating on the Word of God which is the most important step in renewing our mind.
♥ **John 1:1 NIV** *"In the beginning was the Word, and the Word was with God, and the Word was God."*

- ♥ By spending time in the Word, we are spending time with Jesus. We need to allow Him to teach us and show us the *"great and unsearchable things we(you) do not know"* **(Jeremiah 33:3)**

Other influences in renewing our mind:

1) The thoughts we think and the words that we speak.
- ♥ **Proverbs 18:21 NIV** *"The tongue has the power of life and death."*
- ♥ We can determine how situations play out in our lives by the way that we speak and think. Our words have an incredible role in our destinies and the way that we walk out our lives each day.

Thoughts > Words > Actions > Habits > Lifestyle > Destiny

- ♥ Therefore, our thoughts ultimately determine our destiny.

It is so important to renew our minds and to live out the Word of God as our thoughts literally determine our destiny. We must saturate our minds in the Word every day and allow it to influence the way that we think and speak.

2) What we watch and listen too.
- ♥ **Mathew 6:22-23 NIV** *"The eye is the lamp of the body. If your eyes are healthy, your whole body will be full of light. But if your eyes are unhealthy, your whole body will be full of darkness. If then the light within you is darkness, how great is that darkness!"*

- **Romans 10:17 NKJV** *"Faith comes from hearing, and hearing by the Word of God"*
- What we watch has a major impact on our entire being. For example: pornography and horror movies negatively affect our mindsets, wellbeing, and even our relationships.
- What we listen to greatly impacts the way we think. For example: If we are constantly surrounded by negative nellies, it is extremely likely that we will begin to think and speak just like they do.
- Listening to secular music over worship music influences our thinking.

3) The people that we spend our time with.
- It is said that we become our top 5 friends.
- For example: when we spend a lot of time with people who gossip or are very negative, we will likely succumb to their way of living and thinking, even if that wasn't the goal.
- **1 Corinthians 15:33 NLT** *"Don't be fooled by those who say such things, for "bad company corrupts good character."*

It's so important to surround ourselves with people who are just as, or more, hungry for Jesus and for spiritual growth as we are!

However, this is not saying that we shouldn't be loving on these people or ignoring them because we are afraid of their influence in our lives. It's good to spend time with people to show them Jesus, but we should try to not be greatly influenced by their way of living.

4) An attitude of gratitude
- ♥ **Habakkuk 3:17-19 NKJV** *"Though the fig tree may not blossom, Nor fruit be on the vines; Though the labor of the olive may fail, And the fields yield no food; Though the flock may be cut off from the fold, And there be no herds in the stalls- Yet I will rejoice in the Lord, I will joy in the God of my salvation. The Lord is my strength; He will make my feet like deer's feet, And He will make me walk on my high hills."*
- ♥ Even when nothing is going right, it is a CHOICE to rejoice in the Lord. The author of this Scripture commanded his soul to praise the Lord, regardless of his negative circumstances. I'm sure this greatly influenced his way of thinking!

Thanksgiving is usually difficult to practice, yet it opens up the gates of Heaven over our situation. Negativity is a very slippery slope. The moment that we partner with negativity and complaining, it is very difficult to get out of and we begin to believe the negative words that we are speaking. How can God move in our lives when we are only expecting and speaking out bad things? He desires to partner with our gratitude and expectation.

Psalm 116:17 NLT *"I will offer you a sacrifice of thanksgiving and call on the name of the Lord."*
- ♥ It is much easier to complain than it is to rejoice in the Lord. But it bears abundant fruit in our lives and helps in keeping our perspectives on Heaven rather than on our current situation.
- ♥ It helps us to have an eternal perspective.

Mathew 6:33 NKJV *"But seek first the Kingdom of God and His righteousness, and all these things will be added to you."*

♥ We don't have to partner with anxiety, negativity or heavy burdens! We can cast all of our cares, whether big or small, onto Jesus and continue to fix our eyes on the kingdom of God. He will always help us.

Friends, it is important to remember that going to church isn't enough. We need a real relationship with the Father and the renewal of the mind comes as we sit with Him, learn from His ways and listen for His still, small voice. That is where we will learn about His plans for our lives and find help through every difficulty that life can bring.

STORY TIME

I struggled with a pornography addiction for many years. However, when I was baptized in the Spirit, I began to be transformed and empowered to walk in victory over this. Time and time again, when temptation would arise, Holy Spirit would remind me of Ephesians 3:3-4 that states *"But fornication, and all uncleanness of covetousness, let it not even be named among you, as it is fitting for saints; neither filthiness, nor foolish talking, nor coarse jesting, which are not fitting, but rather giving of thanks."* He showed me that the antidote to temptation is thankfulness. The way to combat and exercise authority against the thoughts and desires that tempt us is to begin praising God for all that He has done for us. When we praise God, we enter into the courts of heaven (Psalm100:4), and wickedness can no longer stand in His presence or lead us astray.

PRAY WITH ME:

Dear Heavenly Father,

Thank you that I already have the victory in you because of what You paid for on the cross. Help me to not conform to the pattern of this world, but that I would be totally transformed by the renewing of my mind so that I can be able to test and approve what Your perfect will for my life is. Help me to learn Your will and to yield to You with all that I am. I pray that You would help me to turn away from any negative influences in my life and to keep my eyes filled with light. I ask that You'd sanctify and purify me according to your word and give me clean hands and a pure heart, so that I can be holy and blameless before you in love.

In Jesus Name,

Amen

PERSONAL APPLICATION QUESTIONS

Are your influences (friends, music, movies, etc.) benefiting your life or hurting you?

_____

_____

_____

_____

_____

_____

_____

Is the way that you are living now going to help you get to that place?

_____

_____

_____

_____

_____

_____

_____

What do you hope your life will be like in ten years?

_____

_____

_____

_____

_____

_____

What changes can you make in your life that will help you to grow in character, faith and personal goals?

_____

_____

_____

_____

_____

_____

_____

DEVOTIONAL 2
ROOTED: RELIGION VS RELATIONSHIP

There is a big difference between religion and relationship with Jesus. While we are all called to the service of the gospel, our main priority should always be to walk in friendship and humility with Christ above all things. Below we will explore some verses that demonstrate God's desire to get to know us personally as we walk in relationship with Him. I will conclude with a personal testimony, a prayer and some application questions.

Mathew 26:6-13 TPT *"Then Jesus went to Bethany, to the home of Simon, a man Jesus had healed of leprosy. A woman came into the house, holding an alabaster flask filled with expensive, fragrant oil. She came right to Jesus, and in a lavish gesture of devotion, she poured out the costly oil, and it cascaded over his head as he was at the table. When the disciples saw this, they were offended. "What a total waste!" they grumbled. "We could have sold it for a great deal of money and given it to the poor."*

Jesus knew their thoughts and said to them, "Why are you critical of this woman? She has done a beautiful act of kindness for me. You will always have someone poor whom you can help, but you will not always have me. When she poured the fragrant oil over me, she was preparing my body for burial. I promise you that as this wonderful gospel spreads all over the world, the story of her lavish devotion to me will be mentioned in memory of her."

❤ Even the disciples judged Mary's great act of worship since they felt that the value of the perfume could have been used in a more practical way. However, the Lord was deeply moved by Mary's heart of devotion toward Him and to this day you cannot read through the New Testament without knowing of Mary's gesture. God's heart is moved by simple and genuine acts of love toward Him as He does not desire our performance, but rather a heart abandoned to Him.

Mathew 11: 7-19 TPT *"As they were leaving, Jesus began to speak to the crowd about John. What kind of man did you see when you went out into the wilderness? Did you expect to see a man who would be easily intimidated? Who was he? Did you expect to see a man decked out in the splendid fashion of the day? Those who wear fancy clothes live like kings in palaces. Or did you encounter a true prophet out in the lonely wilderness? Yes, John was a prophet like those of the past, but he is even more than that! He was the fulfillment of this Scripture:*

See, I am sending my prophetic messenger who will go ahead of me and prepare hearts to receive me.

For I tell you the truth, throughout history there has never been a man who surpasses John the Baptizer. Yet the least of those who now experience heaven's kingdom realm will become even greater than he. From the moment John stepped onto the scene until now, the realm of heaven's kingdom is bursting forth, and passionate people have taken hold of its power. For all the prophets and the Torah prophesied until John appeared. If you can receive this truth, John is the Elijah who was destined to come. So listen and understand what I'm telling you. "How could I describe the people of this generation? You're like children playing games on the playground, yelling at their playmates, 'You don't like it when we want to play Wedding! And you don't like it when we want to play Funeral! You will neither dance nor mourn. Why is it that when John came to you, neither feasting nor drinking wine, you said, "Look at this man! He is nothing but a glutton and a drunkard! He spends all his time with tax collectors and other sinners.' But God's wisdom will become visible by those who embrace it."

♥ John the Baptist prepared the way of the Lord by his radical devotion and abandonment to Him, surpassing all of the religious laws of his day. The Bible describes that It was this radical devotion that prepared the way of the Lord. Similarly, the Church today prepares the way for Christ's second coming by our lavish gestures of devotion to the Lord. This happens as we have lives that are totally laid down to Him and His purposes.

Mark 3:13-15 TPT *"Afterward, Jesus went up on a mountainside and called to Himself the men He wanted to be His close companions, so they went up with Him. He appointed the Twelve, who He named the apostles. He wanted them to be continually at His side as His friends, and so that He could send them out to preach and have authority to heal and to cast out demons."*

♥ Friendship with Jesus gave the disciples authority. He wanted them to be continually at His side so that He then could send them out with the authority and power that they required to do mighty things for the Kingdom. Authority only comes when we walk closely with our Savior.

Read **Mark 7:1-23**

Mark 7:5-7 TPT *"So the Pharisees and religious scholars asked Jesus, "Why don't your disciples live according to the age-old traditions passed down by our elders? They should first ceremonially wash their hands before eating." Jesus replied, "You are hypocrites! How accurately did Isaiah prophesy about you phonies when he said: "These people honour me with their words while their hearts run far from me! Their worship is nothing more than a charade! For they continue to insist that their man-made traditions are equal to the instructions of God."*

♥ Jesus hates religion. He would rather your heart be saturated in His love than for you to live by man-made traditions and laws. His first command is to love Him with our whole being. He commands us to do this before he says anything about honouring our mothers and fathers, not lying, stealing, killing, etc.

Psalm 51:16 NLT *"You do not delight in sacrifice, or I would bring it; you do not take pleasure in burnt offerings. The sacrifices of God are a broken spirit; a broken and a contrite spirit; a broken and repentant heart, O God."*

♥ Even David who lived in a time when sacrifices needed to be made to cover mankind's continual disobedience to a lawbook that was impossible to keep, knew that God desires a pure and repentant heart above sacrifice.

1 Samuel 15:22 *"But Samuel declared: "Does the Lord delight in burnt offering and sacrifices as much as in obeying the Lord? To obey is better than sacrifice, and to heed is better than the fat of rams."*
- ♥ Jesus was committed to destroying religious traditions while He walked the earth. He loves to demonstrate to people that He desires friendship over slavery.

Hosea 6: NIV *"For I desire mercy, not sacrifice, and acknowledgment of God rather than burnt offerings."*

Mathew 9:13 NLT *"Now go and learn the meaning of this Scripture: 'I want you to show mercy, not offer sacrifices.' For I have come to call not those who think they are righteous, but those who know they are sinners."*
- ♥ The religious may think that their actions will save them, but they won't since salvation is a gift by God's grace alone. He loves us regardless of what we do and as we walk closely alongside Him we will become like Him. We cannot go from glory to glory by our own strength or by doing all the "right" things.
- ♥ We can't earn salvation or righteousness because it is given to us through grace.

Read **Luke 10:38-42** about Mary and Martha
- ♥ Martha still loved Jesus and welcomed Him into her home but was pulled away from His presence because of many distractions. He asks if her responsibilities were more important than being with Him and states that the best thing to do is to sit at His feet.
- ♥ We often tend to think that we need to serve and perform for God's approval, but God

greatly desires for us to simply sit with Him and be in His presence. This is the most important thing.

Mathew 6:33 TPT *"So above all, constantly seek God's kingdom and His righteousness, then all these less important things will be given to you abundantly."*
♥ As we seek Him, everything else He has in store for us will come to us naturally. Seek His face and He will give you the desires of your heart and supernaturally work all things together as we set our focus on the Kingdom of God.

Read **Luke 15** about the prodigal son.
♥ In this parable the younger brother pursues self-discovery while the older brother is attempting to earn favour from his father. Both needed a revelation of God's grace.
♥ The eldest son was consistently trying to prove himself to his dad through his actions and loyalty when the father's love was unconditional and could not be earned.
♥ It is a choice to live in the freedom of knowing that we are loved like this and that nothing can separate us from the love of the Father. This knowledge leads us to run deeper into the arms of the Father because we know we are safe with Him.
♥ We must know who we are as sons and daughters.

Mark 12:30-31 NIV *"Love the Lord your God with all your heart and with all your soul and with all your mind and with all your strength. The second is this:*

"Love your neighbour as yourself.' There is no commandment greater than these."
- ♥ The first command is to love the Lord with everything that we have, not to love others. Our first priority should always be to love the Lord first and allow our service and love for others to then flow from that place.

John 15:4-5 NKJV *"Abide in Me, and I in you. As a branch cannot bear fruit of itself, unless it abides in the vine, neither can you, unless you abide in Me. I am the vine, you are the branches. He who abides in Me, and I in him, bears much fruit; for without Me you can do nothing."*
- ♥ We can only bear good fruit when we are abiding in His Presence. Anything done apart from Him is of no value, so we must remain in communion with Him.

STORY TIME

One day after moving to a new city, starting a ministry, and being in full-time university I was anxious over many things. Concerned with how I would balance all my responsibilities with excellence, I sat before the Lord and word vomited all of my worries onto His feet. I remember my mind being so dizzy with concern and anxious thoughts that I was completely forgetting to simply listen for the sound of His voice. It was in the middle of a sentence where the Holy Spirit stopped me as I felt His sweet Presence fill my room and quiet my mind. I then heard a gentle whisper say to me *"I just want to spend time with you."*

The Lord was already aware of my needs and concerns. He knew that there was a lot on my plate and that I wanted to do everything with excellence. In that moment He knew that what I needed was just to be still in His Presence and hear from Him, as He went before me to pave the way for all He was calling me to do in this new season.

God knows that we desire to serve Him, but He doesn't want us to be distracted by this. What God desires more than anything is simple friendship with us, and for us to sit at His feet and be with Him.

PRAY WITH ME:

Dear Heavenly Father,

Thank you for desiring friendship with me before anything else. Teach me how to abide in Your love and to do all things out of this place. Thank you that when I abide in You, I can ask whatever I desire and it will be done for me. I pray that you would teach me how to pray and how to hear your voice. I pray that if there is anything taking your place in my heart and life, that you'd help me to remove it.
I love You, Lord.

In Jesus name,

Amen

PERSONAL APPLICATION QUESTIONS

Has there been times in your life where you have found yourself striving for approval from God or man?

_____

_____

_____

_____

_____

_____

_____

Do you think that you could be making more time to spend in God's word every day?

_____

_____

_____

_____

_____

_____

DEVOTIONAL 3
ROOTED: OBEDIENCE

Obedience to God's leading is not often an easy process. It requires surrender, humility and trust in Him to believe that He knows what He's doing and is working all things together for good in our lives. This devotion will help the believer to navigate how to yield to God and His word a bit better each day. I will conclude with a testimony, a prayer and some personal application questions.

Romans 8:14-16 TPT *"The mature children of God are those who are moved by the impulses of the Holy Spirit. And you did not receive the "spirit of religious duty," leading you back into the fear of never being good enough. But you have received the "Spirit of full acceptance," enfolding you into the family of God. And you will never feel orphaned, for as he rises up within us, our spirits join Him in saying the words of tender affection, "Beloved Father!" For the Holy Spirit makes God's fatherhood real to us as he whispers into our innermost being, "You are God's most beloved child!"*

Romans 8:5-9 TPT *"Those who are motivated by the flesh only pursue what benefits themselves. But those who live by the impulses of the Holy Spirit are motivated to pursue spiritual realities. For the sense and reason of the flesh is death, but the mindset controlled by the Spirit finds life and peace. In fact, the mind-set focused on the flesh fights God's plan and refuses to submit to his direction, because it cannot! For no matter how hard they try, God finds no pleasure* *with those who are controlled by the flesh. But when the Spirit of Christ empowers your life, you are not dominated by the flesh but by the Spirit. And if you are not joined to the Spirit of the Anointed One, you are not of Him."*

- ♥ Submit yourselves to God, not out of religious duty in fear of not being good enough, but out of full acceptance as a son/daughter of God.
- ♥ Being responsive to the Spirit helps us to pursue His kingdom and walk out the call of God in our lives.
- ♥ Meditating on the Word of God helps us to hear what the Spirit of the Lord is saying and to keep our minds renewed everyday so that we can be motivated by Him and not our flesh.
- ♥ It is very difficult to walk in obedience when we are focused on ourselves.
- ♥ Our motivations change when our mindset is not focused on our fleshly desires but rather His Kingdom. It becomes easier to walk in obedience when our minds are renewed and set on loving God with all that we have.

John 10:27-28 NKJV *"My sheep hear my voice, and I know them, and they follow me."*

- ♥ In following God, we need to hear His voice. We learn His voice and get to know Him by spending time with Him, just like any relationship.
- ♥ God wants to know us more than we want to know Him.
- ♥ When you make yourself available to the Lord, by positioning yourself near Him on a regular basis, you will naturally grow in your ability to hear His voice.

Isaiah 30:21 NIV *"Whether you turn right or left, your ears will hear a voice behind you saying, "This is the way; walk in it."*
- ♥ His Holy Spirit leads us in the way that we should go, it is up to us to yield to His voice.

Romans 8:12-14 TPT *"So then, beloved ones, the flesh has no claims on us at all, and we have no further obligation to live in obedience to it. For when you live controlled by the flesh, you are about to die. But if the life of the Spirit puts to death the corrupt ways of the flesh, we then taste abundant life."*
- ♥ We are no longer slaves to sin and because of this we do not need to submit to sin but instead to the ways of righteousness.
- ♥ It is a choice to turn away from sin, as we learn to walk in obedience to God

Romans 8:28-32 TPT *"So we are convinced that every detail of our lives is continually woven together for good, for we are his lovers who have been called to fulfill his designed purpose. For he knew all about us before we were born and he destined us from the beginning to share the likeness of his Son. This means the Son is the oldest among a vast family of brothers and sisters who will become just like Him. Having determined our destiny ahead of time, he called us to Himself and transferred his perfect righteousness to everyone He called. And those who possess His perfect righteousness he co-glorified with His Son."*

- ♥ God knows our destiny because He designed it, but its fulfillment requires our full abandonment to Him. We must remain in Him and be yielded to His voice. A fulfilled purpose in Him requires a fully surrendered life that's willing to make sacrifices and walk in radical obedience to His instructions.

♥　Holy Spirit intercedes on our behalf for us to accomplish what we've been assigned to do in our lives. If He knows our destiny and we have Him living within us, we then have a full-time guide that simply requires us to yield our footsteps to His voice.

Mathew 16:24 NIV *"Then Jesus said to His disciples, "Whoever wants to be my disciple, must deny themselves and take up their cross and follow me."*

♥　Walking with Jesus requires a continual "yes" to His leading. It means laying down everything we are holding onto and following Him.

♥　This is a joyful surrender, because when we lay down our lives, we gain the Kingdom of God.

Revelation 3:16 TPT *"So, because you are lukewarm- neither hot nor cold- I am about to spit you out of my mouth!"*

♥　Our purpose is ultimately to live in friendship with Him, and everything else we do is just a biproduct of this relationship. It is so important that we don't become lukewarm in faith since we are called to a life of radical obedience to God!

Romans 8:27 TPT *"God, the searcher of our hearts, knows fully our longings, yet He also understands the desires of the spirit, because the Holy Spirit passionately pleads before God for us, His holy ones, in perfect harmony with God's plan and our destiny."*

♥　He knows our longings better than we do and will reveal to us these godly desires as we yield our lives to Him.

♥　He is a perfect Father and delights to give us good gifts. As we seek Him, He gives us the desires of our hearts in His perfect timing and way. It's so important to understand that He is not a God that withholds from us, but He loves to bless us.

❤ **Romans 8:28 NIV** *"And we know that in all things God works for the good of those who love Him, and are called according to His purpose"*

Most of the time, obedience to God's leading is not an easy process. It requires surrender, humility and trust to know that He always knows better and is working everything together for good even if it doesn't make sense in the moment.

Ephesians 2:10 TPT *"We have become His poetry, a re-created people that will fulfill the destiny He has given each of us, for we are joined to Jesus, the Anointed One. Even before we were born, God planned in advance our destiny and the good works we do to fulfill it."*

❤ Our good works make up our destiny. As we yield to God, our prearranged destiny comes to pass and we are rewarded for simply doing what He set aside for us to accomplish.

❤ He simply requires our yes and He does the rest. We can trust that as we walk close to Him, He will fulfill our lives' purpose. It's HIM who works through us, not our own strength.

Luke 16:10 NIV *"Whoever can be trusted with very little can also be trusted with much, and whoever is dishonest with very little will also be dishonest with much."*

❤ It's important that we are good stewards of the mundane daily tasks that He places in front of us, so that He can trust us with much more.

STORY TIME

Years ago, I knew I was about to embark on a new adventure by moving to the city of Calgary for university. The issue was that I had no idea where I would live or how I would be able to pay for rent each month. My original plan was to stay at the job I was working until the end of the summer, and then move a couple of days before school started, but the Lord changed my plans. I remember asking Him one morning what day I should move and felt like He had said "July 15th". Keeping in mind that this was a full month's worth of pay that I was losing and that I still had no place to stay. This made me really nervous and even though I didn't fully understand why, I decided that it was better to be obedient and trust the Lord than to be disobedient by staying longer.

After I said "yes" to God, it was within the span of a couple weeks that my dad ended up moving to Calgary in the same part of town as my university and for the entire time that I lived at his place, I was blessed with free rent. Once I got to Calgary, it was within the first week of being there that I met some of my best friends and was offered a couple of amazing opportunities that I likely would have missed out on if I had stayed longer in my hometown. I learnt through this that even though God's leading may not make sense to us in the moment, His thoughts are so much higher than ours and He always leads us in the right direction when we choose to trust in Him.

Proverbs 3:5-6 NIV *"Trust in the Lord with all your heart and lean not on your own understanding. In all your ways submit to Him and He will make your paths straight."*

PRAY WITH ME:

Dear Heavenly Father,

Thank you that You work everything together for the good of those that love You. Thank you that we can trust you as You call us to yield to Your voice. Thank you that Your thoughts are not my thoughts, and Your ways are not my ways. Help me to trust you and surrender my will to follow You to the best of my ability.

In Jesus Name,

Amen.

PERSONAL APPLICATION QUESTIONS

What does it look like to walk in simple obedience to God in the day to day?

_____

_____

_____

_____

_____

_____

_____

Is there any big or small area of your life that God is asking you to say "yes" to Him in?

_____

_____

_____

_____

_____

_____

_____

Is saying "yes" to God always easy? Why?

_____

_____

_____

_____

_____

_____

_____

Can you think of a situation that God would ask you to be obedient in saying "no"?

_____

_____

_____

_____

_____

_____

_____

DEVOTIONAL 4
ROOTED: FAITH, TRUST & REST IN HIM

Waiting on the Lord is not an easy process and requires us to place all of our trust in Him. The Bible promises that those who wait on the Lord will not be ashamed, (Psalm 25:3) and He is faithful to fulfill every word that He has spoken. In the process of trusting the Lord in faith to see Him come through on our behalf, contentment in Him is key and can help us along the way. This devotion offers wisdom on how to have faith in God's promises through trust and contentment in Him. I will conclude with a personal testimony, a prayer, and some application questions.

Mathew 6:33 NIV *"But seek first the Kingdom of God and His righteousness, and all these things will be given to you as well."*

Mathew 6:10 NIV *"Your Kingdom come, Your will be done on earth as it is in Heaven."*

♥ It is important to understand that the Lord knows what He is doing, even when it doesn't make sense to us in the natural or turn out the way that we thought it would.

♥ In **1 Peter 5:7 NIV** it says to *"Cast all your anxiety on Him, because He cares for you."*

♥ We can be worry free about what is to come because as we seek Him above all other things, He works it all together for good according to His perfect will for our lives.

Romans 8:28 NKJV *"And we know that all things work together for good to those who love God, to those who are called according to His purpose."*

♥   When we truly seek God with all of our hearts, it frees us to rest in His will for our lives, as we are lead to experience His goodness in a greater way.

Ephesians 3:20 TPT *"Never doubt God's mighty power to work in you and accomplish all this. He will achieve infinitely more than your greatest request, your most unbelievable dream, and exceed your wildest imagination! He will outdo them all, for his miraculous power constantly energizes you."*

♥   The Word says that He does immeasurably more than we can ask or imagine, so we can trust and believe that He is doing bigger and better things than we can perceive behind the scenes.

♥   It might not always work out as we expected, but God promises to do more than what we may have thought He would.

Isaiah 55:11 NKJV *"So shall My word be that goes forth from My mouth; It shall not return to Me void, but it shall accomplish what I please, and it shall prosper in the thing for which I sent it."*

♥   It is important to believe the promises God gives us through His word. His word is truth, so we can trust that what He says He'll do, He will do. He doesn't speak unless He plans to fulfill His words.

♥   For example, Romans 8:28 is a promise from God. We can trust and declare this truth over our lives that God always works everything together for good to those who love Him. He wouldn't speak this if He wasn't going to be faithful to it.

Ezekiel 12:25 NKJV *"For I am the Lord. I speak, and the word which I speak will come to pass; it will no more be postponed; for in your days, O rebellious house, I will say the word and perform it," says the Lord God."*

♥ He keeps His promises, and He does what He says He will do.

♥ People may break their promises to us, but *"God is not a man that He should lie; nor a son of man, that He should repent. Has He said, and will He not do? Or has He spoken, and will He not make it good?"* **Numbers 23:19 NKJV**

Psalm 144:4 NKJV *"Man is like a breath; His days are like a passing shadow."*

♥ Our lives on earth are very temporary and every man is a vapour in the scheme of eternity. It is important to remember that during our short time on earth, every answer to prayer is to bring God glory and praise.

♥ Our answered prayer requests testify to God's goodness. We can trust Him to answer our prayers in His perfect timing, knowing it will give Him glory.

2 Corinthians 4:17 TPT *"We view our slight, short-lived troubles in the light of eternity. We see our difficulties as the substance that produces for us an eternal, weighty glory far beyond all comparison."*

♥ This can help us to rest in God's timing because we know that in eternity, every prayer request will be answered and we will experience a glory that is beyond comparison to what we know now.

Hebrews 6:19 NIV *"We have this hope as an anchor for the soul, firm and secure."*

♥ Our hope is in knowing that we are already victorious and get to spend eternity in God's presence.

♥ We will likely face many trials during our lives but can rest assured in knowing that we not only have the Holy Spirit living within us, but also get to spend eternity with God.

Psalm 91:1-2 NKJV *"He who dwells in the secret place of the Most High shall abide under the shadow of the Almighty. I will say of the Lord, "He is my refuge and my fortress; My God, in Him I will trust."*

♥ When we dwell in His presence and seek His face, we are hidden under His shadow. No evil can touch us because we are insulated, isolated and incubated by His Holy Presence. He is our safe place and we can trust in Him and His mighty ways.

Psalm 27:4-5 NKJV *"One thing I have desired of the Lord, that will I seek: that I may dwell in the house of the Lord all the days of my life, to behold the beauty of the Lord, and to inquire in His temple. For in the time of trouble He shall hide me in His pavilion; in the secret place of His tabernacle He shall hide me; He shall set me high upon a rock."*

♥ It is a good thing to present our requests to God, but we should not be seeking them above deeply knowing and loving Him. It is important to not get caught up in seeking the things we *need* from God and forget to seek Him first in friendship.

♥ Trusting in God often becomes a lot easier when our relationship with Him satisfies us fully, and we don't need other things to satisfy our souls.

♥ It is in the secret place that we are set high upon a rock. It's hard to see clearly when we don't sit down with the Father and learn His nature and His ways.

Psalm 63:1 NKJV *"O God, You are my God; early will I seek You; my soul thirsts for You; my flesh longs for You in a dry and thirsty land where there is no water."*
♥ David writes this while in the wilderness of Judah. He had no food and water yet states that He is hungry and thirsty for God alone.
♥ God is the only one who can satisfy the very longing of our soul; Him. David recognized that no answer to prayer could fully satisfy Him but that He needed more of God.

Psalm 107:9 NKJV *"For He satisfies the longing soul, and the hungry soul with goodness."*
♥ What happens when we receive our answer to prayer? We will always have another prayer request, but our souls will not be satisfied unless we continue to commune with God.

Psalm 16:11 NIV *"You make known to me the path of life; You will fill me with joy in your presence, with eternal pleasures at your right hand."*

♥ There is so much more of God to experience than only seeking Him for what He can do for us. As beloved children of God, it's so important that we are seeking Him to really KNOW Him. It grieves the heart of the Father when we try to use Him only for His benefits, when these things are a biproduct of being in closeness to Him.
♥ In Heaven, miracles won't matter any longer. Your devotion to Him on Earth however, will.
♥ Don't get me wrong, the Father delights to give us the desires of our hearts and wonderful gifts, but

none of those things matter in comparison to walking in friendship and intimacy with Him.

Read **Mathew 26:36-45**
♥   **Verse 39 NIV** *"Going a little farther, He fell with His face to the ground and prayed, "My Father, if it is possible, may this cup be taken from me. Yet not as I will, but as you will."*
♥   Effective prayer happens when we pray His will alone, and not our own. In the garden of Gethsemane, Jesus prays the Father's will, even though He is God and can essentially do whatever He wants too.
♥   God worked all things together for good, and Christ's momentary sufferings produced an eternal glory that was far greater than could have been imagined.
♥   He does this in our lives as well, working all things together for our good and His glory. Even when the process doesn't make sense and it seems that God may not be answering our cries, He is doing a mighty work in our lives and in the end we will have the opportunity to praise God.
♥   Just like Jesus, we must find our strength in God alone, for apart from Him we can do nothing. (John 15:5)

Mathew 5:3 NIV *"Blessed are the poor in spirit, for theirs is the kingdom of heaven."*
♥   Being poor in spirit also means to be humble and totally dependent on God for everything.
♥   Other words for *'blessed'* are: enriched, happy, fortunate, delighted, blissful, content.

Romans 5:3-5 TPT *"Even in times of trouble we have a joyful confidence, knowing that our pressures will* *develop in us patient endurance. And patient endurance will refine our character, and proven character leads us back to hope. And this hope is not a disappointing fantasy, because we can now experience the endless love of God cascading into our hearts through the Holy Spirit who lives in us!"*

♥   Faith is a tool that God loves to use to lead us to completely depend on Him and not our own strength.

♥   Patience in trials and waiting for God to do something in faith, helps us to grow in character and relationship with God. He is more concerned with the process of transforming us than the result of our prayers. If we always got what we wanted right away, it might be difficult to grow in our faith as it requires us to have none.

♥   Faith is more about perfecting you on the inside and bringing you closer to Him than it is about fixing things instantly on the outside.

♥   The enemy may try to get you to give in to doubt and lies by telling you that God doesn't care and isn't capable of fulfilling His word, but this simply is not true. God uses our faith journey to bring us from glory to glory. (2 Corinthians 3:18) This is why we must press into Him in the secret place and learn what He's truly like, so that we don't fall away from Him during trials.

Mathew 5:4 TPT *"What delight comes to you when you wait upon the Lord! For you will find what you long for. "*

Genesis 21:1-3 NLT *"The Lord kept his word and did for Sarah exactly what he had promised. She became pregnant, and she gave birth to a son for Abraham in* *his old age. **This happened at just the time God had said it would.*** "(emphasis added)

♥   It may not have occurred in Abraham's timing and he had to wait a lot longer than expected, but God did as He promised. He finished what He started in the appointed timing...and because of it, He got all of the glory rather than Abraham.

Hebrews 11:11 NKJV *"By faith Sarah herself also received strength to conceive seed, and she bore a child when she was past the age, because she judged Him faithful who had promised"*

♥   God is Faithfulness. Just because things don't always happen the way that we think they should, doesn't mean that God isn't faithful to His Word- He just knows much better than our small brains can understand.
♥   **Isaiah 55:8-9 NIV** *"For My thoughts are not your thoughts, neither are your ways My ways," declares the Lord. As the heavens are higher than the earth, so are my ways higher than your ways and My thoughts than your thoughts."*

Hebrews 11:33 TPT *"Their faith fastened onto their promises and pulled them into reality"*
♥   One way to partner with faith is to declare out loud the promises He has given to us. God always honours our belief and trust in Him, He will come through for us in the perfect way!

Hebrews 11:34 TPT *"Although weak, their faith imparted power to make them strong. Faith sparked courage within them and they became mighty warriors in battle, pulling armies from another realm into battle array."*

♥   This is the kind of authority that we can carry as sons and daughters of God. We are warriors who, with God's strength, are mighty in battle and able to pull armies from another realm into battle array.

Hebrews 11:35 TPT *"Faith-filled women saw their dead children raised in resurrection power. Yet it was faith that enabled others to endure great atrocities. They were stretched out on the wheel and tortured and didn't deny their faith in order to be freed, because they longed for a more honorable and glorious resurrection!"*

♥   We are living for eternity and not of this world. Therefore, it is incredibly important that we recognize who we are and WHOSE we are as God's children. When we understand this, we begin to make decisions based on the impact it will make in eternity instead of just during our temporary lives on earth.

♥   Our lives are much more than answered prayers, miracles, money, community, health, etc. Since we live for eternity, all is for His glory alone.

Think of the witnesses that went before us in verses 36 and 37 who were mocked, severely beaten, imprisoned, brutally killed, sawn in two, slaughtered by the sword, lost everything, endured great affliction, and were cruelly mistreated...
Truly the world was not worthy of them, not recognizing who they were."

♥   Most of us will experience trials that are unlike these. However if we are not walking closely in friendship and intimacy with God and we end up facing hardships in life, will our faith still stand?

♥   It's so important that we are allowing Him to search our hearts, refine us and become sufficient for us in all things as we walk close to Him every day.

Hebrews 11:39 TPT *"These were true heroes, commended for their faith, yet they lived in hope without receiving the fullness of what was promised them."*

♥   They were commended for their faith, yet they didn't see the fullness of what they were waiting for.

♥   They stayed faithful to God even though they didn't see God fulfill His promises to them during their lifetimes. This shows us that God is worthy of our obedience and trust even when we don't understand or see the fruition of what He spoke.

♥   Even though He is always faithful to His word, this doesn't necessarily mean that we will see it come to pass in the timing or way that we expect.

♥   An example of an Old Testament hero that is commended for their faith without seeing the fruit of what they were waiting for is King David. He deeply desired to build a temple for the Lord's presence to dwell in. (1 Chronicles 17:2) Yet God decided to allow David's son Solomon to oversee this work rather than David (verses 11-12) This is because God wanted a man of peace to build His house rather than a man who had shed so much blood during battle. In 1 Chronicles 17:26-27, David offers God praise even though He wouldn't see the temple built how he thought, it was still a tremendous blessing that God would allow His son to establish it. David still got to help with gathering materials and preparing plans for the temple's construction, however the building of the temple occurred differently than he had expected.

Hebrews 11:40 TPT *"But now God has invited us to live in something better than what they had- faith's fullness! This is so that they could be brought to finished perfection alongside of us"*

♥ God has all the ability to answer our prayers and He actually wants to. Since Jesus already paid the highest price for our sin on the cross, what else would He withhold from us? He delights to give us good and perfect gifts.

♥ When we wait on God in faith, it is perfected in us as we learn to trust fully in Him and love Him above all other things.

♥ He knows better than we do, therefore the process of waiting in faith might look different than we expected it would. It's so important that we are learning to trust Him in the process and remember that nothing is impossible with Him. (Luke 1:37)

What is faith?
As **Hebrews 11:1 NKJV** describes, *"Now faith is the substance of things hoped for, the evidence of things not seen."*

Hebrews 12:1 TPT *"So we must let go of every wound that has pierced us and the sin we so easily fall into. Then we will be able to run life's marathon race with passion and determination, for the path has already been marked out for us."*

♥ This race will not be easy, but the proper path has been marked out before us.

♥ When we have wounds within us that are undealt with, this can weigh us down and withhold us from running our race with freedom. It is important to deal with the pain that we have on the inside by the help of the Holy Spirit.

♥ One way that we can do this is through forgiveness. This can be a very hard process to go through when we are choosing to forgive the people that have hurt us, but it is necessary if we want to walk in true freedom.

♥ If you have a close friend, or someone that you can trust, it may be helpful to walk through forgiveness with someone that will be a safe presence for you to process through it with.

♥ It's easy to blame God for the bad things that have happened to us. However, the reality is that we live in a fallen world filled with individuals that are free to make their own decisions aside from God. He is very different from man and wants to comfort you when you are in need.

♥ The verse above mentions the sin that easily entangles us and the context would point to the sin of disbelief and doubting God's promises. When we doubt, this can hold us back from running our race with passion and determination.

Hebrews 12:2 NKJV "Looking unto Jesus, the author and finisher of our faith, who for the joy that was set before Him endured the cross, despising the shame, and has sat down at the right hand of the throne of God."

♥ If He is the author, the perfector AND the finisher of the faith within us, then He can do what He wants to do in the process.

Proverbs 3:11-12 NKJV *"My son, do not despise the chastening of the Lord, nor detest His correction; for whom the Lord loves He corrects, just as a father the son in whom he delights."*

♥ It's so important for our growth as Christians that we fully embrace God's correction as part of our training. The things that we endure can help to shape our character and mature us.

♥ When we are corrected by the Father, it shows that we are living as genuine sons and daughters of God.

♥   Having a healthy fear of the Lord leads us to be holy as He is holy and helps us to see God rightly.

Refer to **Genesis 5:32-10:1**
♥   Think of Noah who did not see any fruit of God's word for years, but He remained faithful to the Lord who fulfilled His word in the perfect way and timing.

Psalm 62:5 NKJV *"My soul, wait silently for God alone, for my expectation comes from Him."*
♥   He knows best! Let Him set our expectations as we seek His face.

Jeremiah 17:7 NKJV *"Blessed is the man who trusts in Him and whose hope is in the Lord."*
♥   Blessed is the one who trusts in nothing (examples: a dream, vision, person, money) but God alone.

Isaiah 49:23 NKJV *"Then you will know that I am the Lord, for they shall not be ashamed who wait for Me."*
♥   Those who wait on Him will not be ashamed or disappointed.

Galatians 5:6 TPT *"All that matters now is living in the faith that works and expresses itself through love."*
♥   Faith is activated and brought to perfection by love.

John 15:4-5 TPT *"So you must remain in life- union with me, for I remain in life- union with you. For as a branch severed from the vine will not bear fruit, so your life will be fruitless unless you live with your life intimately joined to mine. I am the sprouting vine and you're My branches. As you live in union with me as*

*your source, fruitfulness will stream from within you-
but when you live separated from me you are
powerless."*

♥ Our faith is not perfected unless we are abiding
in the one who IS Love. We must be immersed in His
love and continue to spend time getting to know Him
by seeking Him in the secret place. If we live
separated from Him, it is easy for disbelief to creep
into our lives.

♥ If we live separated from God, then we live
powerless.

John 15:7 TPT *"But if you live in life-union with me
and if my words live powerfully within you, then you
can ask whatever you desire and it will be done for
you"*

♥ We can experience so much more of God
when we live close to Him in friendship. We have
access to everything that Jesus has access too, but
to experience these things requires us to walk in
intimacy with God.

STORY TIME

In 2018, I attended the University of the Nations to complete a six-month discipleship training program. Since it was a very expensive trip, I worked hard for about two years beforehand to save up the money that I needed for the full time that I was there.

However, a week prior to leaving I still had about $2000 that I needed to go fully funded and I had no idea how I was going to make the money on time. Since I had already quit my full-time job to prepare to leave, things weren't looking up for me. I had the option of asking some supporters to help me but in my heart, I wanted to see God come through for me without my interference. For five days straight I prayed and prayed that God would provide for me.

It wasn't until the day before my departure that two friends of mine invited me over to their homes to say goodbye and ended up blessing me with the exact amount that I needed to cover my trip. In His perfect timing, God came through for me at the last moment and I was so glad that I had put my trust in the Lord and got to experience Him work a miracle on my behalf.

PRAY WITH ME:

Dear Heavenly Father,

*You alone are my portion, prize, and inheritance
(Psalm 16:5). I ask that You'd help me to put my trust
in You fully as I wait for You to answer my prayers
according to your perfect will.*

*Your Word says that godliness with contentment is
great gain, (1Timothy 6:6) so please help me to be
content in You.*

*I ask that You'd show me how to have faith for the
things that You've promised in Your Word. Thank You
that You always fulfill the words that You speak.
(Isaiah 55:11) Today I choose to trust You, Lord.*

In Jesus Name,

Amen

PERSONAL APPLICATION QUESTIONS

Has there ever been anyone in your life that has broken a promise to you?

_____

_____

_____

_____

_____

_____

How did that incident affect the way that you understand God's faithfulness?

_____

_____

_____

_____

_____

_____

Is there anything that you are believing God for in this season?

_____

_____

_____

_____

_____

_____

DEVOTIONAL 5
ROOTED: LEARNING TO HEAR HIS VOICE

Hearing God's voice is something that is available for every believer and accessible for all who seek Him. God wants to speak to us. Holy Spirit came on the Day of Pentecost to lead us, fill us, and allow us to commune with the Father and through Him, we can learn how to hear the still, small voice of God. There are many verses that confirm this such as:

John 10:27 NIV *"My sheep listen to My voice; and I know them and they follow Me."*

Romans 10:17 NIV *"Consequently, faith comes from hearing the message, and the message is heard through the word about Christ."*

Isaiah 30:21 TPT *"When you turn to the right or turn to the left, you will hear his voice behind you to guide you, saying, "This is the right path, follow it."*

Luke 11:28 TPT *"But God will bless all who listen to the word of God and carefully obey everything they hear."*

For some, hearing God's voice may come easier than for others, and that's okay. As we grow closer to God in relationship, hearing His voice will become easier to decipher and recognize. Another thing that's important to understand is that everyone may hear God in different ways, such as through the Word. When we read the Word of God, we are communing with God and listening to His voice since **John 1:1** state's that *"the Word was God"*.

We also may hear Him through dreams or visions, in music, in prayer, etc. God is not limited and can speak to us in many different ways.

It is important to define the four different voices that we can hear in order to properly discern the voice of God in our lives.

1. OUR OWN VOICE
♥   Our own imaginations, ideas, desires, thoughts, etc.
♥   *"Lean not on your own understanding."* **Proverbs 3:5-6**
♥   *"He who trusts in himself is a fool."* **Proverbs 28:26; Isaiah 5:21**
♥   When we walk close to the Lord, His desires become our desires. Our mind is renewed and transformed as we grow in friendship and intimacy with God. **Psalm 37:4 TPT**
♥   **Romans 12:2** says that we can actively be renewing our mind, so our thoughts will begin to be a lot more like Jesus' as we grow with Him.
♥   We can give Him our burdens. When we do this, our minds become clearer and able to think rightly.
1 Peter 5:7; Psalm 68:19; Phil.4:6

2. THE VOICE OF OTHERS

♥ Parents, teachers, media, pastors, friends, etc.

♥ When we really trust the people that surround us, it can be easy to trust their voice above the voice of Holy Spirit. However, we should be careful to only look to others as much as they look to Jesus and His Word. Always take everything back to the Lord, even if the advice sounds really great.

♥ It is a healthy thing to have mentors and people around us that can be trusted and can help to counsel us throughout our lives. These people can even help us to discern what voices we are submitting to, by the help of the Holy Spirit.

3. THE VOICE OF THE ENEMY

♥ We can discern that it's the enemy speaking to us when it doesn't align with the Word of God. Are these thoughts causing peace or confusion? Do they stir up strife or lead us into paths of goodness? It's good to ask Holy Spirit to give us discernment so that we can know when it's the enemy speaking instead of God

♥ We can always bring these thoughts back to the Word of God to test them.

♥ *"Submit yourselves, then, to God. Resist the devil, and he will flee from you."* **James 4:7 NIV**

♥ *"Put on the full armor of God, so that you can take your stand against the devil's schemes."* **Ephesians 6:11 NIV**

♥ *"Stand firm against him, and be strong in your faith."* **1 Peter 5:6-11 NLT**

4. **THE VOICE OF GOD**

♥ The purpose of prayer is to grow in relationship with God as You communicate with Him.

♥ It is crucial that we are listening to His voice so that we can walk in friendship and intimacy with Him and be properly guided through our lives.

♥ We are His children (Romans 8:16) and good fathers communicate with their kids. We all have access to this by the Holy Spirit who came so that we could walk in closeness with the Father and have access to Him at all times. It is by His Holy Spirit that we receive wisdom, guidance, counsel, etc.

♥ God is always speaking and anyone that is a part of His family can hear from Him! (John 10:27)

The Lord is more excited to speak to us then we are to hear from Him! We need to learn to tune our ears to hear His voice.

You may be asking, *"How do we learn to hear His voice?"*

Well, <u>PRACTICE!</u>

Practice makes perfect when it comes to hearing from God. It takes time to discern God's voice apart from the others. When you pray, I encourage you to not just tell God what you need, but to make space for Him to speak to you as you are quiet before Him. An activity you can try is to ask Him questions and wait on Him until you hear His answer!

God wants to speak to you not just for information, but to grow in friendship with you. Like I said before, prayer is about growing in relationship through communication.

When I was first learning how to discern God's voice, one thing that I would do to practice hearing was to ask Him to help me find my keys when I would misplace them. Without fail, every time He would tell me exactly where they were and it would blow my mind when I would find them lying there.

Another time, I was working in the drive thru of Tim Hortons chatting with a newly hired employee. We were talking about our heritage and families, when out of the blew she asked me to guess her middle name. She told me that there was no way I would guess it because it was so unusual. Without even asking the Holy Spirit to help, I heard Him whisper her middle name to me. *"Delilah!"* I stated confidently with a smirk on my face. Her mouth almost dropped to the floor as she was so stunned that I got it on the first try. *"How in the world did you know that?!"* she asked me, while pulling me to the locker room to show the proof on her license. I can't say that I used this opportunity to preach the gospel to her, although I wish that I had.

However, it just goes to show that Holy Spirit is present with us and wants to speak to us more than we often realize.

Some other things to consider when growing in listening to God's voice:

1. Making Jesus Lord over your life is the most important and valuable thing that anyone could ever do. Not only as your Saviour, but over every aspect of your life. Are you fully yielded to Him every day and walking in friendship with Him as He leads you in His perfect will for your life? Are you willing to receive His words when He speaks them? Are you willing to make changes in your life when He asks? We are called to follow His will and not our own. (Romans 12:2, 2 Corinthians 5:15)

2. **Mathew 5:8 NIV** says *"Blessed are the pure in heart, for they shall see God"* This shows that having a pure heart is vitally important in communicating with God. He desires to trust us with the mysteries of His heart, but this requires a heart of humility that is willing to sit before Him and hear from Him without an agenda. He is not limited to our agendas, sin, poor motives, etc., but spending this time with Him to simply grow in friendship is very important as we learn to hear His voice.

3. We need to learn to be still. Is your mind running rampant when you sit before Him? Are you full of anxious concerns, distraction, frustration, or agitation? This can be distracting from what He has to say and can hinder us

from hearing His voice. It's important to remember that we have authority to bind distraction and take it captive! (James 4:7)

In these moments, we can ask Holy Spirit for help to lay all distractions down at His feet. I always find it helpful to either pray out loud, sing the Word, use my imagination to picture Jesus or simply to begin thanking and praising Him!

Psalm 100:4 NIV says that we *"enter His gates with thanksgiving and His courts with praise"* therefore, this is a useful way to help get our minds off of other things and back onto Jesus.

4. Holy Spirit loves to help and will always point us to Jesus. We can ask Him to come and fill us, and to teach us how to pray. (Luke 11:1-13, John 16:12-14)

5. Remember that the righteous live by faith and because of this we need to believe that God speaks and have faith to believe when He actually does. We can see in Habakkuk 2:4 that it is by faith that we are able to receive the things that He speaks to us.

6. Every word that we receive should be tested according to the Word of God. (Acts 17:11; 2 Timothy 3:16-17) We can also test these words by whether or not it glorifies God, if it helps to bring us into closer relation with Him, and if it brings us peace and clarity, or confusion, etc.

7. Ask a spirit filled friend or leader that you trust if you need some guidance! It is sometimes necessary and helpful to ask our community for help when we need it.

PERSONAL APPLICATION QUESTIONS

How do you most often hear from God?

_____

_____

_____

_____

_____

_____

_____

Have you ever had an experience where God spoke to you very clearly?

_____

_____

_____

_____

_____

_____

_____

Has there ever been a time where you thought that God was speaking to you but weren't certain because it was difficult to discern the voices?

_____

_____

_____

_____

_____

_____

Is there any way that you can practice hearing God's voice more clearly on a consistent basis?

_____

_____

_____

_____

_____

_____

_____

TIME TO BEAR FRUIT

Now that we have made it through the journey of Arbor Discipleship Training Curriculum, what are you going to do?

He desires for our hearts to be fully yielded to Him, and that we would allow Him to work in and through our lives as we come close to Him in friendship.

John 15:16 NIV says *"You did not choose Me, but I chose you and appointed you that you might go and bear fruit-fruit that will last- and so that whatever you ask in my name the Father will give you."*

You are chosen by God, you are loved by God, you are seen by God, you are heard by God, you are adopted as a child of God, and you are accepted by God. He has a mighty purpose and plan for you (Jeremiah 29:11) and wants you to walk in life abundantly (John 10:10), as a victorious son or daughter (Romans 8:16)!

Friend, I encourage you to take the time to get to know Him every day. He is the best friend, the kindest Father, the Kinsman Redeemer, the Salvation of our souls and He is worthy of it all. I pray that His fire will burn inside your heart *until your surrender to His will for your life doesn't even seem like a sacrifice anymore.* (Song of Songs 8:7)

What has impacted your life as you have journeyed through this curriculum? What have you learned? How have you grown?

_____
_____
_____
_____
_____
_____
_____
_____
_____
_____
_____
_____
_____
_____
_____
_____
_____
_____
_____
_____
_____
_____
_____
_____
_____
_____

Are there any changes that you have made or know that you need to make to help you grow closer to God?

_____

_____

_____

_____

_____

_____

_____

_____

_____

_____

_____

_____

_____

_____

_____

_____

_____

_____

CLOSING PASSAGE TO PONDER

Psalm 139: 1-24 TPT

Lord, you know everything there is to know about me.

You perceive every movement of my heart and soul,

and you understand my every thought before it even

enters my mind.

You are so intimately aware of me, Lord.

You read my heart like an open book

and you know all the words I'm about to speak

before I even start a sentence!

You know every step I will take before my journey even

begins.

You've gone into my future to prepare the way,

and in kindness you follow behind me

to spare me from the harm of my past.

With your hand of love upon my life,

you impart a blessing to me.

This is just too wonderful, deep, and incomprehensible!

Your understanding of me brings me wonder and strength.

Where could I go from your Spirit?

Where could I run and hide from your face?

If I go up to heaven, you're there!

If I go down to the realm of the dead, you're there too!

If I fly with wings into the shining dawn, you're there!

If I fly into the radiant sunset, you're there waiting!

Wherever I go, your hand will guide me;

your strength will empower me.
It's impossible to disappear from you
or to ask the darkness to hide me,
for your presence is everywhere, bringing light into my
night.
There is no such thing as darkness with you.
The night, to you, is as bright as the day;
there's no difference between the two.
You formed my innermost being, shaping my delicate
inside
and my intricate outside,
and wove them all together in my mother's womb.
I thank you, God, for making me so mysteriously complex!
Everything you do is marvelously breathtaking.
It simply amazes me to think about it!
How thoroughly you know me, Lord!
You even formed every bone in my body
when you created me in the secret place,
carefully, skillfully shaping me from nothing to something.
You saw who you created me to be before I became me!
Before I'd ever seen the light of day,
the number of days you planned for me
were already recorded in your book.
Every single moment you are thinking of me!
How precious and wonderful to consider
that you cherish me constantly in your every thought!

O God, your desires toward me are more
than the grains of sand on every shore!
When I awake each morning, you're still with me.
O God, come and slay these bloodthirsty, murderous men
For I cry out, "Depart from me, you wicked ones!"
See how they blaspheme your sacred name
and lift up themselves against you, but all in vain!
Lord, can't you see how I despise those who despise you?

ABOUT THE AUTHOR

Kaylee Farn lives in Alberta, Canada. She is passionate about training the church to walk in wholeness, identity, and intimacy with God. She is the co-founder of a ministry called *Queens* that trains and equips women for a lifestyle of revival. She has been trained under multiple ministries including *Royal Identity Ministries* and *Youth With a Mission*. She also has a blog, *To Her Beloved,* that she uses as a platform to encourage the Church.

Made in the USA
Middletown, DE
28 September 2021